Quest to Learn

This report was made possible by grants from the John D. and Catherine T. MacArthur Foundation in connection with its grant-making initiative on Digital Media and Learning. For more information on the initiative, visit www.macfound.org.

The John D. and Catherine T. MacArthur Foundation Reports on Digital Media and Learning

Peer Participation and Software: What Mozilla Has to Teach Government by David R. Booth

The Future of Learning Institutions in a Digital Age by Cathy N. Davidson and David Theo Goldberg with the assistance of Zoë Marie Jones

The Future of Thinking: Learning Institutions in a Digital Age by Cathy N. Davidson and David Theo Goldberg with the assistance of Zoë Marie Jones

Kids and Credibility: An Empirical Examination of Youth, Digital Media Use, and Information Credibility by Andrew J. Flanagin and Miriam Metzger with Ethan Hartsell, Alex Markov, Ryan Medders, Rebekah Pure, and Elisia Choi

New Digital Media and Learning as an Emerging Area and "Worked Examples" as One Way Forward by James Paul Gee

Living and Learning with New Media: Summary of Findings from the Digital Youth Project by Mizuko Ito, Heather Horst, Matteo Bittanti, danah boyd, Becky Herr-Stephenson, Patricia G. Lange, C. J. Pascoe, and Laura Robinson with Sonja Baumer, Rachel Cody, Dilan Mahendran, Katynka Z. Martínez, Dan Perkel, Christo Sims, and Lisa Tripp

Young People, Ethics, and the New Digital Media: A Synthesis from the GoodPlay Project by Carrie James with Katie Davis, Andrea Flores, John M. Francis, Lindsay Pettingill, Margaret Rundle, and Howard Gardner

Confronting the Challenges of Participatory Culture: Media Education for the 21st Century by Henry Jenkins (P.I.) with Ravi Purushotma, Margaret Weigel, Katie Clinton, and Alice J. Robison

The Civic Potential of Video Games by Joseph Kahne, Ellen Middaugh, and Chris Evans

Quest to Learn: Developing the School for Digital Kids by Katie Salen, Robert Torres, Loretta Wolozin, Rebecca Rufo-Tepper, and Arana Shapiro

Quest to Learn

Developing the School for Digital Kids

Katie Salen, Robert Torres, Loretta Wolozin, Rebecca Rufo-Tepper, and Arana Shapiro

The MIT Press
Cambridge, Massachusetts
London, England

This book was set in Stone Serif and Stone Sans by the MIT Press.

Library of Congress Cataloging-in-Publication Data
Quest to learn : developing the school for digital kids / Katie Salen . . . [et al.].
     p.   cm. — (The John D. and Catherine T. MacArthur Foundation reports on digital media and learning)
Includes bibliographical references.
ISBN 978-0-262-51565-8 (pbk. : alk. paper)
1. Information technology—Study and teaching—United States.
2. Computers--Study and teaching—United States. 3. Internet in education—Australia—United States. I. Salen, Katie.
LB1028.5.Q84   2011   371.33'44678—dc22   2010015788

Contents

Series Foreword

The John D. and Catherine T. MacArthur Foundation Reports on Digital Media and Learning, published by the MIT Press, in collaboration with the Monterey Institute for Technology and Education (MITE), present findings from current research on how young people learn, play, socialize and participate in civic life. The Reports result from research projects funded by the MacArthur Foundation as part of its $50 million initiative in digital media and learning. They are published openly online (as well as in print) in order to support broad dissemination and to stimulate further research in the field.

Preface

Game designers traffic in the space of possibility. They design systems that define rules and thus give rise both to play and to a sense that anything is possible. As a game designer, I believe in the value of such spaces. The design of Quest to Learn thus began with an inquiry into the idea of possibility.

What, for example, my team asked, might be made possible for *kids* if we found a way to conceive of school as just one kind of learning space within a network of learning spaces that spans in school, out of school, local and global, physical and digital, teacher led and peer driven, individual and collaborative?

What might be made possible for *teachers* if their creativity around how to engage kids were deeply valued and they were supported with resources—such as collaborating with game designers—to really understand what engagement around learning can look like?

What might be made possible for *communities* if school were to become a catalyst for activating a network of mentors, partners, peers, and leaders who are focused on helping kids figure out how to be inventors, designers, innovators, and problem solvers?

What might be made possible for *students* if they were challenged to teach others how to do the stuff they know how to do, and content were treated as an actionable resource rather than something to be memorized?

What might be made possible if young people not only were able to use games and media and models and simulations as drivers of their learning, but were able to *design* them, too?

What might be made possible for the *world* if we were able to support young people to be curious, to have ideas and build theories around those ideas, to fail often and early as a strategy for learning how something really works, to be given an opportunity to interact with the larger world in ways that feel relevant, exciting, and empowering?

What might be made possible if we treated *school* not just as a problem to be fixed or complained about, but as a partner in the learning lives of our kids, our parents, and our communities? What might actually be possible?

New York City was willing to hedge its bets and see what would be possible when a school stops talking about technology as a learning solution and instead looks to young people as the centers of innovation. Quest to Learn is the result of this bet, a new sixth- to twelve-grade public school that opened its doors in fall 2009 with 76 extremely excited sixth graders.

In the pages that follow, you'll see the design thinking behind the details that led to this excitement, but it is important to be clear about something now in order to address any possible misconceptions. Quest to Learn is not a school of video games or a school where students play video games all day. Games are one important tool in the school, most certainly, but they represent something more than a resource. They are the basis of a theory of learning that is both situated and gamelike. As a result, we have designed the school around an approach to learning that draws from what we know games do best: drop players into inquiry-based, complex problem spaces that are scaffolded to deliver just-in-time learning and to use data to help players understand how they are doing, what they need to work on, and where to go next. It is an approach that creates, above all else, a need to know—a need to ask, Why and how and with whom?

In this first semester, for example, our sixth graders have been involved in a code-breaking Mission where they were motivated to learn how to convert fractions into decimals in order to break a particularly gnarly piece of code they found hidden in one of their library books. They were also recruited by a TV producer to create a location guide for a reality television series, a situation that created in them a need to figure out how to navigate an atlas, distinguish elements of a map, and create character studies for potential contestants. Several students asked for additional reading so that they might see some more examples of characters to draw from. They demanded to learn how to create more professional-looking video tutorials to help a hapless group of fictional inventors known as the Troggles, who live in a video game called *LittleBigPlanet*, learn the purpose of standardized measurement.

In the case of the Troggles, the students' need to know came directly from an interest in helping others learn. And they are deeply engaged in learning how to do this teaching of others well in order that they may claim they know the content, too.

Further, the curriculum at Quest to Learn creates feedback loops that connect intentionally redundant and overlapping learning opportunities, like the after-school program called Mobo Studio, which supports students in learning how to create videos, an integrated math/science class where the creation of video tutorials is the primary form of summative assessment, and which includes a specially designed social-network platform called Being Me, allowing students to post, rate, and review each others tutorials and video remixes against assessment-oriented rubrics.

This kind of feedback loop—one made up of various learning contexts across which kids move—is almost always reinforcing. The kids have opportunities to practice and synthesize content and skills in varied contexts that have been intentionally designed to point to other spaces to learn.

And then there is the *rise*. Structures and experiences emerge from the system because attention has been paid to the possibilities the spaces afford. Feedback loops act like connective tissue between the "bone" of state standards and core literacies. And when designed well, feedback loops can give rise to the kinds of supplementary, passion-based learning we know help young people excel.

Case in point: on the third day of class, the YouTube Club emerged, which now has 24 members. This club has assigned itself the job of "telling the story" of the school in mockumentary format. With more than two-thirds of the school year left to go, there is no end in sight to what the students will dream up next.

We need to do a better job of giving children and young people opportunities to rise, which means designing systems that enable the rise—that enable them to move across networks and to engage in really hard problems with relevant resources.

Games are all about creating spaces of possibility, where players feel that they can do anything. I believe schools can aspire to design these kinds of spaces, too.

Katie Salen
Executive Director of Design
Quest to Learn
www.q2l.org
Professor, Design and Technology
Parsons the New School for Design
December 2009

About This Document

This research-and-development document outlines a learning framework for Quest to Learn, a sixth- to twelfth-grade small school in New York City that opened its doors to its first sixth grade class in the fall of 2009. The school was designed by the Institute of Play in partnership with New Visions for Public Schools, the largest education-reform organization in New York City dedicated to improving the quality of education children receive in New York City's public schools. The school is scheduled to add a subsequent grade each year after 2009.

The goal of this document, written in spring 2008, was to share the initial design with a broad community of experts for comment and feedback. The document focuses on research and design development and includes draft samples of our approach to curriculum and assessment and an overall structure of the school's design. Please note that much of the focus of the document is on the sixth-grade experience because that is the grade that opened first in fall 2009. We developed these components over a period of eight months. This document should therefore be read as the seminal document in a school design process, but it has also been edited and revised to fit its publication in the MacArthur Foundation series. We will continue to grow our development team as we work with teachers, parents, and others outside the school. We recognize the role of parents and community as integral to the school's success and have developed specific opportunities for them and both current and prospective students to voice their concerns as we move forward.

Our school design process attempts to harness strategic thinking around gaming and game design as an innovative curricular and learning paradigm and actively seeks to change the way institutions of learning are conceived of and built.

Ten Core Practices Defining Quest to Learn

Taking on Identities
My identity as a learner is complex and evolves with my membership in my own community of practice. I am a writer, designer, reader, producer, teacher, student, and gamer.

Using Game Design and Systems Thinking
Everything I do in school connects to my life outside of school through a game design and systems perspective.

Practicing in Context
School is a practice space where the life systems I inhabit and share with others are modeled, designed, taken apart, reengineered, and gamed as ways of knowing.

Playing and Reflecting
I play games and reflect on my learning within them.

Theorizing and Testing
I am learning as I propose, test, play with, and validate theories about the world.

Responding to a Need to Know
I am motivated to ask hard questions, to look for complex answers, and to take on the responsibility to imagine solutions with others.

Interacting with Others

Games are not only a model for helping me think about how the world works, but also a dynamic medium through which to engage socially and to develop a deeper understanding of myself in the world.

Experimenting and Imagining Possibilities

I take risks, make meaning, and act creatively and resourcefully within many different kinds of systems.

Giving and Receiving Feedback

My learning is visible to me, and I know how to anticipate what I will need to learn next.

Inventing Solutions

I solve problems using a game design and systems methodology: I identify the rules, invent a process, execute, and evaluate.

Glossary

The Annex   An extended Mission prep period to hone literacy and math skills.

Being Me   A school-based social-network site where students can communicate, post work, collaborate, and reflect.

Being, Space, and Place   A class connecting social studies with reading and writing fiction, nonfiction, poetry, and comics.

Boss Level   Two-week "intensive" where students apply acquired knowledge and skills to propose solutions to complex problems.

Codeworlds   A class where math meets English language arts and language rules the day.

Home Base   10 kids + one very interested adult = student advisories that meet twice a day.

Institute of Play   Quest to Learn's founding partner.

Mission Lab   Quest to Learn's game design and curriculum development studio.

Missions (Discovery Missions)   10-week units that give students a complex problem they must solve.

Q2L   Quest to Learn

Quests   Challenge-based lessons that make up Missions.

SMALLab Mixed-reality learning lab focused on embodied learning.

Smartool A "tool to think with" that students create as part of their class work.

Sports for the Mind A class focused on digital media, game design, and systems thinking.

State Standards Content and skills that the state of New York has determined every student should know.

The Way Things Work A science and math class where students learn how to take all kinds of systems apart and put them back together again.

Wellness A class designed to get students moving and thinking about ways to be healthy—including everything from nutrition to sports to mental, social, and emotional health.

Quest to Learn

Background

This chapter offers an overview of the motivations and implications for the creation of Quest to Learn (Q2L). In addition to outlining a particular set of needs that the school is attempting to respond to and innovate around, this background also describes the design and development process used in the creation of this document.

The Seed of an Idea

In 2006, the MacArthur Foundation turned its attention to the design of twenty-first-century learning environments that would respond to the needs of kids growing up in a digital, information-rich, globally complex era prizing creativity, innovation, and resourcefulness. As part of this work, in spring 2007 New Visions for Public Schools joined forces with Katie Salen (Center for Transformative Media, Parsons the New School for Design, and Institute of Play, a games and learning nonprofit) in developing an idea for a school that would use "gamelike learning" as a way to empower and engage students from all walks of life. Q2L is the result of this collaboration and is specific in its focus on connecting student learning to the demands of the twenty-first century and on supporting young people in their learning across digital networks, peer communities, content, careers, and media. The school is being designed to help students bridge old and new literacies through learning about the world as a set of interconnected systems. Design and innovation are two big ideas for the school, as is a commitment to deep content learning with a strong focus on learning in engaging, relevant ways. The school is a place where digital media meets books and where students learn to think like designers, inventors, mathematicians, and more. Q2L brings together teachers with a passion for content, a vision for helping kids to learn best, and a commitment to changing the way students will grow in the world.

Motivation and Implications

The ideas suggested by Q2L are critical to the future of public education in New York City and elsewhere. All young people today need high-quality education more than ever before. Success in the twenty-first century requires mastery of high-school-level mathematics, written and oral communications skills, and the abilities to solve problems, to work as a member of a team, and to use technology. The preservation of democracy in a diverse country demands that schools give children and youth experiences and knowledge that will build the civic competencies of tolerance, intergroup communication, conflict resolution, and engagement in public life.

In too many urban areas, however, the predominant mode of public education—the large comprehensive high school of the 1950s and 1960s—and, more important, the curriculum and pedagogy of those schools are outdated and cannot enable every student to meet high academic standards or gain these skills. Too many students in these schools are unengaged and disconnected, and they see no purpose in their education. There are no opportunities for these students to assume responsibility for significant portions of their own education. They drift through schools staffed by poorly trained teachers, sit in large classes with little inquiry, hands-on experiences, or encouragement to reflect critically, and exist in anonymity among their teachers and many of their peers. These schools are ill equipped to address key academic challenges confronting urban students: personal social and developmental issues, the increasing complexity of material they are expected to learn, and their own alienation from school.

A Need for Innovation

Q2L has emerged at a time when there is a dire lack of American educational models designed to prepare learners for the innovations needed in twenty-first century. The number of U.S. citizens completing science and engineering degrees declines each year. In China, 59 percent of undergraduate students receive degrees in these fields; in Japan, 66 percent do; in the United States, however, only 32 percent do (Shaffer 2006). Thirty years ago the United States ranked third worldwide in the number of science and engineering degrees earned each year; today it ranks seventeenth. Approximately 60,000 U.S. high school students enter the prestigious Intel International Science Fair each year, but that is a small number compared to *6 million* entrants from China (Shaffer 2006). A recent Trends in International Mathematics and Science Study report indicated that 7 percent of U.S. students scored at the most advanced levels in math, whereas in Singapore 44 percent of students did (Friedman 2006). Worse yet, almost-one third of all students drop out of school in the United States, and only 50 percent of Latino, African American, and Native American students in the United States complete high school (Greene 2002). According to a recent Gates Foundation–funded study, 81 percent of those who drop out of school claim that "opportunities for real world learning" would have improved their chances of staying in school, 69 percent were "not inspired to work hard," and 47 percent said that "classes were not interesting." Significant to these findings was also the fact that *only* 35 percent of those interviewed claimed that they left because they were "failing in school" (Bridgeland, DiIulio, and Morison 2006, 4, 7). Taken together, these findings speak directly to the levels of alienation from learning that high school dropouts experience as a result of schooling.

In the meantime, although many students are alienated from school, other data show that their uses of digital media have increased. In March 2005, the Kaiser Family Foundation released a report that found that, on average, youth of both sexes between the ages of 8 and 18 are exposed to 8 hours and 33 minutes (8:33) of digital and other media (defined as the Internet, music, video games, television, and movies) *daily*, black

youth to 10 hours and 10 minutes (10:10) daily, and Latino
youth to 8 hours and 52 minutes (8:52). Of those hours, black
youth spend an average of 1 hour and 26 minutes playing video
games daily; Latino youth, 1 hour and 10 minutes; and white
youth, 1 hour and 3 minutes (Roberts, Foehr, and Rideout 2005,
7). Also in 2005, a study by the Pew Internet and American Life
project reported that 57 percent, or about 12 million, of online
teens between the ages of 12 and 17 are content creators of such
things as blogs; a personal Web page; a Web page for a school,
a friend, or an organization; original artwork, photos, stories, or
videos; remixed content that forms a new creation (Lenhardt
and Madden 2005, 8). Interestingly, of these content creators,
urban and lower-income youth were more likely than their suburban and rural counterparts to engage in these activities. For
example, 36 percent of youth who lived in households with an
annual income of $30,000 or less created online content com-
pared to the 35 percent of youth who lived in households earning from $30,000 to $50,000. The percentage for youth living in
households earning $50,000 or higher decreased slightly (Len-
hardt and Madden 2005, 12).

This is not to say, however, that we are close to closing the
digital divide or, more aptly, "the participation gap," as Henry
Jenkins and his colleagues (Jenkins, Clinton, Purushotma, et al.
2006) call it. Although significant gains have been made in providing minimal access to a computer and the Internet to most
youth in schools and libraries, up-to-date technologies continue
to move faster than these institutions have been able to sustain.
Lower-income communities lag considerably in their acquisition of computers and high-speed connectivity. Also, as Jenkins

and his coauthors explain, accessing technology has become less important than accessing the skills and content necessary to participate in fast-evolving technological trends. Whereas accessing books, visiting museums, and going to concerts used to draw the line between the social practices of middle- and low-income communities, access to technologies and their related social online experiences is now playing a similar role in today's society.

In the past five years, New York City's small-school movement has begun to address these conditions by creating more than 100 secondary schools that function as caring environments where students are known and can excel with one another. Early success is particularly evident through high graduation rates—79 percent for 2006 and 76 percent for 2007—from the first two cohorts of New Visions' New Century High Schools. And this rate is particularly impressive because these schools serve some of New York City's lowest-performing, underserved incoming ninth graders each year. As the most recent evaluation by Policy Studies Associates reveals, "Available data show that students educated in [New Century High [S]chools in 2004–05 were better prepared for graduation than comparable students in traditional schools. All precursors—attendance rates, credit accumulation, promotion rates, and the number of Regents exams passed—pointed in the right direction" (Policy Studies Associates 2006, 61).[1]

Games and game-based pedagogy build on these strengths of small schools and promise to create new, more effective classroom learning strategies that creatively engage students in the questions associated with learning complex material and reengaging with schools. Q2L, through its support of gamelike learning, can incorporate key findings from youth development literature about the environmental factors that greatly increase student resiliency and increase the chances for academic and social success of youth living in high-risk environments. These factors include high expectations of students' abilities and skills; participation in activities that engage their voluntary commitment; opportunities to make contributions and to have these contributions recognized and assessed; and continuity of support. It is critical that students foster these skills not only to succeed in school, but also ultimately to succeed in college and the work world.

Our Design and Development Process

Members of a small core team—Katie Salen, Rebecca Rufo-Tepper, Arana Shapiro, Robert Torres, and Loretta Wolozin—with support from New Visions staff, including Gloria Rakovic and Ron Chaluisan, have led the development of the Q2L learning framework. Curriculum and teaching experts from a range of areas were consulted and will have an expanded and ongoing role. We have worked with middle school students from the Ross Global Academy throughout the process to date and will extend our reach to students and teachers across the New York City Department of Education (DOE) network as Q2L grows. In addition, the development process has included a range of partners who bring innovation and credibility to the work, including:

The Institute of Play   As the founding partner, the Institute of Play is driving the design of the school framework, leveraging its expertise in the design of learning systems and the uses of games and its work with a range of audiences around games and their design. The institute is staffed by professional game designers and leading researchers in the fields of game-based pedagogy, new media literacies, the learning sciences, assessment, and youth development. It is responsible for the design of Q2L, providing research support, curriculum, and assessment expertise and piloting models for the school as part of the school design process.

Parsons the New School for Design   Parsons is providing support and resources related to student recruitment and research work around SMALLab, a mixed-reality learning lab housed in the school.

New Visions for Public Schools   New Visions is providing guidance and staff resources related to the design and oversight of the school and supervised the final development of this proposal for submission to the New York City DOE in November 2008.

New York City DOE   Bruce Lai, the DOE's chief technology officer, is lending support to the work through facilitating outreach to various school leaders, teachers, and students within the DOE. This facilitation has allowed the Q2L design team to include a range of stakeholder voices in the design process.

MacArthur Foundation Digital Media and Learning Network   A MacArthur Foundation planning grant has enabled our team to work with a number of experts in the fields of learning, assessment, and literacy. Key individuals among these experts include:

▪ Nichole Pinkard, University of Chicago, Center for Urban School Improvement

- Jim Gee, Mary Lou Fulton Professor of Literacy Studies at Arizona State University
- Daniel Schwartz, Stanford University School of Education
- Alice Robison, New Media Literacies Project, MIT
- Connie Yowell, John D. and Catherine T. MacArthur Foundation

The school development team will continue to expand to include parents, students, leaders in the community where the school is located, and a group of expert teachers to lead the curriculum development effort.

Note

1. *Evaluation of the New Century High Schools Initiative: Report on the Third Year.* Policy Studies Associates, March 31, 2006, 61.

Mission

Opening with the question, "What makes Quest to Learn unique?" this chapter goes on to describe a set of skills, concepts, literacies, and ways of knowing that shape the school's situated approach to teaching and learning.

What Makes Quest to Learn Unique?

The learning that takes place at Q2L is situated and gamelike. By "situated," we mean that students are asked to "take on" the identities and behaviors of designers, inventors, writers, historians, mathematicians, and scientists in contexts that are real or meaningful to them or both. By "gamelike," we mean an approach to learning that draws on the intrinsic qualities of games and their design to engage students in a deep exploration of subject matter, with twenty-first-century learning at its core. These qualities come from an understanding that

- Games are carefully designed, learner-driven systems.
- Games produce meaning.

- Games are dynamic systems.
- Games are immersive.
- Games are interactive and dynamic, requiring a player's participation.
- Games instantiate worlds in which players grow, receive constant feedback, and develop ways of thinking and seeing the world (Salen 2007b).

The internal architecture of games—rules, components, core mechanics, goals, conflict, choice, and space—guide the design of learning experiences. Thus, throughout the Q2L curriculum, game design is used as a learning strategy for students. Game design requires high levels of complex thinking to ensure that a host of elements interact to offer players meaningful and lasting engagement. Q2L capitalizes on current games, learning, assessment, and game design research; the chapter titled "Game-Based Learning and Knowing" provides further discussion of Q2L's underpinnings in the contemporary learning sciences field.

Q2L aims to create a learning environment for students in which they act within situated learning contexts to solve complex problems in math, science, English language arts (ELA), and social studies in gamelike ways. Integrated learning contexts provide practice space for goal-oriented challenges. Work with models, simulations, and games through an evidence-based inquiry curriculum serves as the foundation for the study of dynamic systems and their effects. The curriculum supports students in developing a way of thinking about global dynamics, for example: how world economic, political, technological, environmental, and social systems work and are interdependent across nations and regions. High levels of student engagement and ownership in the learning process are valued as students participate in a rigorous process of research, theory building, hypothesis testing, evaluation, and critique, followed by a public defense of results.

Ongoing evaluation and feedback create opportunities for students to plan, iterate, and reflect on their own learning. The overall curriculum is rooted in mathematical practices, with an explicit intent to innovate at the level of how students are assessed in context. Value is placed on work within cross-functional teams where students contribute specialized practices to solve a problem collaboratively. Game design—for either digital or nondigital contexts—provides a platform for students to explore a range of ideas and to build systems to be experienced by others. Most important, the bar to student achievement is set high, with the expectation that students and teachers together will gain the skills necessary to meet these requirements and even surpass them.

Attention to the development of academic and civic practices takes place through an integrated curriculum and situated assessment scheme. In addition to immersion in basic literacy practices—reading, writing, and calculating—the focus at Q2L is on dynamic "ways of knowing and doing," such as the ability to think, read, and interact critically; to solve complex problems in mathematics and science; and to express oneself persuasively as author, agent, and consumer through language and media. Students learn to reflect on and act within feedback loops connecting the school and life systems found in the social, technological, and natural worlds they inhabit (Schön 1987). An

integrated health and wellness program supplements this globally focused curriculum.

Where Is School?

At Q2L, the design of learning takes into account the creation
of pathways between experiences, communities, and contexts,
and it reconsiders "school" as just one node within a larger
network of learning spaces within and across which students
move. Rather than defining school as a separate place in time
and space from the concerns and communities of children's
lives, Q2L defines it as a social landscape that reaches into the
home as well as into the local and global communities to which
students belong. This does not mean that students are expected
to be "at school" 24/7; it does mean that all experiences are
considered potential contexts for learning.

In the figure "Snapshots of a Student's Life," several kinds of
learning spaces are identified: home, lab (before- and after-school
spaces located in proximity to the school building), school Day
("formal" space of the school), global communities (social networks, virtual worlds, etc.), and local communities (soccer team,
neighborhood library, youth club, and so on). Certain experiences might connect across home and lab, for example, as when
a student reads anime at home and with friends and is in the
Anime Club as part of lab. The network is extended when the
student joins an online fan-fiction site around a favorite author.

We see learning as *practice* and Q2L as a *practice space*. The
more spaces, communities, and contexts that students gain experience in as practitioners of learning, the stronger they will grow.

Snapshot of a Student's Life

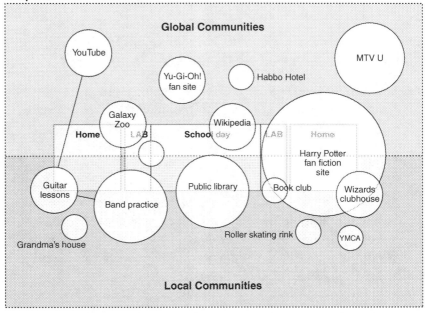

Ways of Knowing

The Q2L pedagogy involves a melding of technological, social, communicational, scientific, and creative concerns, including:

▪ *Systems-Based Thinking*   Students design and analyze dynamic systems, a characteristic activity in both the media and in science today.

▪ *Design Thinking*   Students apply design methods as strategies for innovation to both problem-solving and problem-seeking activities.

• *Interdisciplinary Thinking* Students solve simple and complex problems that require them to seek out and synthesize knowledge from different domains. They become intelligent and resourceful as they learn how to find and use information in meaningful ways.

• *User-Centered Design* Students act as sociotechnical engineers, thinking about how people interact with systems and how systems shape both competitive and collaborative social interaction.

• *Specialist Language* Students learn to use complex technical linguistic and symbolic elements from a variety of domains, at a variety of different levels, and for a variety of different purposes.

• *Metalevel Reflection* Students learn to explicate and defend their ideas, describe issues and interactions at a metalevel, create and test hypotheses, and reflect on the impact of their solutions on others.

• *Network Literacy* Students learn how to integrate knowledge from multiple sources, including music, video, online databases, other media, and other students. In doing so, they participate in the kinds of collaboration that new communication and information technologies enable.

• *Productive/Tool Literacy* Students gain an ability to use digital technologies to produce both meanings and tangible artifacts, including games.

A Gamelike Curriculum

Learning at Q2L takes place within an integrated curriculum that has a foundation in math and science and is designed to align with New York State standards. Discovery Missions—

questlike challenges that require students to plan, collect data, create theories, test their results, and document outcomes—structure student movement within specially designed learning contexts. Discovery Missions require students to analyze, build, and modify many different kinds of dynamic systems—historical, physical, mathematical, technological, scientific, written, and social. Through Missions, students are supported in both thinking and doing, and they develop an orientation toward innovation and creativity as well as a fluency in foundational numeracy and comprehension literacies. Discovery Missions are covered in detail in the chapter titled "Curriculum Structure."

In addition to supporting learning that is situated (see "Game-Based Learning and Knowing"), the Q2L Mission-Quest curriculum quite naturally integrates learning within a social world. While students develop their own work, engaging in a wide range of gamelike learning experiences, they also connect with other students in the school community, both to share expertise and to play together via the building of solutions. Situating learning within a community of learners is critical because one of our pedagogical goals is that students achieve a degree of mastery in practice; immersion in a community of learners engaged in authentic versions of such mastery-driven practices is therefore required.

Five Conditions for Student Learning

The Q2L curriculum activates five conditions for student learning: a need to know, a need to share and reflect, an occasion to share, a context for ongoing feedback and evaluation, and

channels for distribution across internal and external communities. *A need to know* means creating learning environments
that support situated inquiry and discovery so that students
have rich contexts within which to practice with concepts and
content. *A need to share and reflect* means that opportunities
for critical feedback and collaboration are built into the design
of any learning experience. *An occasion to share* represents the
need for teachers and students alike to create specific contexts
for reflective interaction or opportunities for students to share
their knowledge and get feedback on their work. The creation
of *a context for ongoing feedback and evaluation* refers to the
integrated and situated nature of assessment within the Q2L
model—all learning experiences provide learners with continual
and transparent feedback on achievement toward goals. Last,
channels for distribution across internal and external communities
create infrastructures for students to share their work, skill, and
knowledge with others. These channels might take the form of
online public portfolios, streamed video or pod casts, student-
led parent conferences, or public events where work is critiqued
and displayed, to name but a few such infrastructures. Within
the curriculum, game design, games, models, and simulations
serve not only as potential gateways into certain kinds of technology or design expertise, but also as contexts for mastery
of skills such as collaborative learning, conflict resolution,
systems-based thinking, planning, and the ethics of fair play.

The Quest to Learn Community

Students and teachers sit at the heart of any school community. This chapter profiles the qualities of each, emphasizing the emergence of these qualities from a set of core values defining the school.

Quest to Learn Student Profile

Q2L's main goal is that every student who graduates will possess the knowledge, skills, and habits of mind necessary to succeed and contribute in the twenty-first-century global environment. In the attempt to define what students will know and do upon graduation, we considered not only content-based knowledge, but also those situated practices and literacies that students need to use this knowledge in a way that is meaningful to them. If students cannot act in and with the knowledge they gain in school, they cannot persist in crafting their own identities as independent learners. Q2L therefore strives to create the conditions where connections to everyday experience are celebrated, internalized, and demonstrated across all aspects of the school.

Q2L graduates will be prepared to engage in postsecondary education and lifelong learning in a rapidly changing global environment because of the attributes we strive to produce in them.

Academically Prepared
Each Q2L graduate will

- Be prepared for the requirements of matriculation for standard, postsecondary school experiences.
- Have earned a high school diploma with course credits sufficient for entry into any state's university system.
- Have mastered the content and practices necessary to engage successfully in postsecondary coursework and to complete a college degree or other postsecondary certification.
- Be proficient in a language other than English.

Able to Recognize and Recruit Different Ways of Knowing
Each Q2L graduate will

- Have experienced the world as a set of interconnected systems and learned strategies for acting within these systems in ways that are relevant and empowering.
- Have gained experience in achieving integrated expertise: researching, theorizing about, demonstrating, and revising new knowledge about the world and the systems of which it is composed. Graduates will be able to use this expertise within future contexts as demands require.
- Have mastered essential principles of game design in multiple contexts for multiple purposes.
- Have developed a way of thinking about global dynamics: how world economic, political, technological, environmental, and

social systems work and how they are interdependent across nations and regions.

Able to Recognize and Recruit a Range of Learning Practices
Each Q2L graduate will

- Recruit relevant ways of knowing for learning in particular contexts.
- Use models and simulations to understand and predict the behavior of systems, in math, science, geography, and computation.
- Use game design and system thinking as lenses through which to view society and culture as well as through which to express ideas and emotions.
- Reason and problem-solve as part of understanding the goals of a system; engage complex problems; collect, analyze, and synthesize information from a range of sources; tolerate ambiguity and uncertainty; and apply appropriate ways of knowing to produce potentially viable solutions.
- Recruit appropriate resources and practices essential to comprehend, analyze, evaluate, develop, and present information in an articulate, persuasive, and appropriate manner for specific purposes—through speech, with visual demonstrations, in writing, and through games and digital communication tools in a manner that demonstrates awareness of diverse points of reference.
- Be fluent in a range of technology practices—able to use essential computer and technological tools for communication, presentation, and data analysis and to adapt such skills to relevant technologies as they emerge.

- Consume games, media, arts, information, and technology with a critical perspective engaged and be able to evaluate sources of bias, validity, and scholarly integrity.
- Be intellectually curious and able to plan for, organize, and evaluate learning opportunities for lifelong learning.
- Be able to work in collaborative, cross-functional teams.
- Recognize his or her own areas of mastery and can contribute this knowledge toward work with others on complex, multidimensional problems.
- Think, read, and interact critically to solve complex problems in mathematical and scientific contexts.
- Express himself or herself persuasively through language and evidence-based reasoning.

Is an Engaged and Purposeful Citizen
Each Q2L graduate will

- Be a thoughtful, well-informed citizen who is able to take and value cultural perspectives other than his or her own to construct a multidimensional understanding of the natural world and human experience.
- Be a collaborative player who understands how to work and learn with individuals who hold varied points of view and who bring different resources to bear on the problem at hand.
- Be able to design play and other kinds of systems for a range of audiences, recognizing the need to choose appropriate language, behaviors, and strategies of interaction.
- Understand the factors influencing his or her personal health and wellness and be able to make informed choices to enhance his or her overall physical, mental, and emotional health.

- Demonstrate ethical decision-making skills and be able to make responsible choices for the benefit of himself or herself and others and for the development of a more just and peaceful world.

Student Resources

Students not only will develop these capacities within the curricular experiences of the school but will be supported in their development through internships, community service, service-learning opportunities, and capstone research projects, especially within the upper grades. The Q2L curriculum, combined with cocurricular and extracurricular support, develops the aforementioned abilities, capacities, and dispositions in students. In addition, it seeks to draw on the community resources within the neighborhood where it is located as well as on organizations throughout New York City and the world to enrich the curriculum and enhance students' learning experiences. The Institute of Play provides game design and development expertise for students and teachers and serves as a primary conduit to the professional game-development community. Student development over time is to be documented within multiple, overlapping systems, including an online social-network space (Being Me) and annual portfolios.

Student Support Structures

Students' social, physical, cognitive, and emotional development are always a consideration in developing daily curriculum and are explicitly addressed in student support structures. These structures include an ongoing advisory program in which all staff support students in developing strategies to manage their identities as students, peers, and young people. Students open and close each day with a small advisory group known as Home Base, which is led by a teacher. Home Base lasts 10 to 15 minutes and provides opportunities for students and teachers to come together to deal with the daily concerns of adolescents before these concerns become more serious issues for students. Advisory groups are small—10 students to 1 teacher—and thus create opportunities for teachers to develop strong mentoring relationships with students. Because the groups are small, teachers are responsible for monitoring academic or behavioral issues that arise, referring students on an as-needed basis to a student support team most likely consisting of a counselor, intervention specialist, other Q2L teachers, and administrators. The support team will determine together the appropriate interventions for individual students who are having problems that their teacher-adviser cannot handle alone.

Teachers

Q2L's experienced teachers share the school's vision for game-based learning and academic rigor. They have the desire to work collaboratively, the experience in doing so, and the capacity to integrate game design and systems-based content, issues, and perspectives with state standards. In addition, ongoing professional development is an integral part of teaching at Q2L. Faculty will continue to work with the Institute of Play to develop curriculum and resources for use by the students and to create a learning environment in which students are supported in the design of curriculum for other students. Ninth-grade Q2L students, for example, may design games for use in the sixth-grade curriculum or by their own peers. In addition, throughout each semester teachers will participate in study groups, lesson study, and peer observation, and daily common planning time will allow for meaningful collaboration.

Flexible scheduling enables teachers to work in teams to collaborate on the design of an integrated curriculum. Longer instructional periods (75 to 90 minutes) make in-depth projects and experiences possible. Thematic curriculum fosters cross-discipline connections and facilitates the development of critical thinking, making, and reasoning skills. Smaller class size (25 students) enables students to develop strong relationships with school staff and gives teachers the opportunity to create varied and differentiated learning opportunities. An instructional team of teachers and administrators also supports the faculty in differentiating instruction to meet the needs of English-language learners and special-education students. This team shares strategies and resources with all staff and helps teachers to modify instruction based on students' individual needs.

Profile of a Quest to Learn Teacher

Student success at Q2L depends greatly on the teachers we hire. Our teachers help shape and sustain the school's vision, mentor and support the students in their learning, and contribute to a deeper understanding of the opportunities and challenges of a game-based learning model. As such, we have developed a teacher profile that offers both a vision and a standard toward which each Q2L staff member can pursue his or her own goals as a teacher and a researcher and create professional development plans to meet these goals. We expect our teachers, like our students, to have areas of strength and weakness as well as areas of growth and interest to which they are committed. As such, no teacher can meet all criteria of the profile, but there is an expectation that our teachers will continually work toward excellence and overall balance in the skills they bring through their practice.

In addition to meeting appropriate New York City DOE and New York State DOE licensure and certification requirements for subject and grade levels, teachers who join the Q2L learning community operate within a specific profile.

Fluent in Gamelike Approaches to Learning

A Q2L teacher

• Understands and engages in complex problems; collects, analyzes, and synthesizes information from a range of sources; tolerates ambiguity and uncertainty and supports students in pursuit of the same.
• Effectively models the essential skills of reading, writing, comprehending, analyzing, listening, speaking, and designing necessary for student learning.
• Sees himself or herself as a learner, writer, designer, reader, producer, student, and gamer.
• Creates contexts with and for students to connect to relevant resources in ways that strengthen the school's systems-based focus.

- Is committed to creating situated-learning experiences for the students.
- Is an innovative, systems-oriented thinker who models thinking and reasoning practices for students within evidence-based contexts.
- Is an integrative and effective user of games, models, and simulations.
- Is enthusiastic about working in a collaborative-learning community where teachers are empowered to take on multiple roles, including leadership and administrative roles.

Youth Focused
A Q2L teacher is

- Committed to student development and the success of all students.
- Responsive to feedback and able to modify methods to ensure the effectiveness of the learning environment for students on an ongoing basis.
- An excellent communicator, listener, and mentor.
- Sensitive to diverse students' varied needs.
- Metareflective and able to recognize and act on the needs of individual students, colleagues, and the school community.
- An advisor and advocate for students.
- Able to evaluate, select, and use various forms of games, media, and technology in lesson design and implementation to maximize student learning.

Academically Prepared
A Q2L teacher

• Has a deep understanding of his or her own content expertise and can connect this expertise to that of others within applied-learning contexts.

• Is intellectually curious and possesses a commitment to life-long learning.

• Is fluent in use of technologies to communicate and work across time, space, and place to extend contexts for student learning.

• Continually models and creates opportunities for students to coengage in reflection on their own learning.

• Uses game design and systems-based learning to provide contexts for inquiry and discovery, leading students to engage actively in their own learning. Through this method, students actively analyze, manipulate, and evaluate information and media, construct knowledge, and solve complex problems in individual and collaborative settings.

Responsible, Civically Engaged, Ethical

A Q2L teacher is

• Committed to behaving ethically toward all members of the learning community.

• Responsible in the decisions he or she makes that affect the learning community and has an understanding of the potential outcomes of these decisions on local, national, and global levels.

• Able to model forms of civic engagement for students that demonstrate an understanding of the role that individual voices and communities can play in shaping the quality and value of life.

• Responsible and committed to helping each student achieve excellence.

- Receptive to others' perspectives; welcoming of differences in interpretation and judgment; and able to revise and expand his or her own views.
- A dedicated member of the Q2L professional community and participates in ongoing professional development, including lesson study, peer review and mentoring, study pods, and networking with teachers locally, nationally, and internationally.

Game-Based Learning and Knowing

The design of Q2L has been informed by recent research and findings in the learning sciences, game studies, and educational reform methods. This section offers an overview of foundational ideas, including precedents and a rationale for a situated-assessment model.

History

The link between games and learning is not a contemporary phenomenon or a digital one. Long before *Quest Atlantis* or *Oregon Trail* hit the market, games were used as learning tools. Members of the volunteer Militia of Rhode Island played American Kriegsspiel in the years following the Civil War; theater games such as Sibling Rivalry were used in contexts ranging from activism to acting; and Friedrich Fröebel's invention of kindergarten in 1840 was premised in large part on the integration of learning, games, and play (Salen 2007a). Attempts to use computer technologies to enhance learning began with the efforts of pioneers such as Richard Atkinson, Mona Morningstar, and Patrick Suppes in 1968; the presence of computer technology in classrooms has increased dramatically since that time, including the use of games and simulations.

As a result of rapid changes in the way technology interacts with almost all aspects of contemporary life, today we live in the presence of a generation of kids who have known no time untouched by the promises and pitfalls of digital technology. Born into a world where concepts such as copyright, mastery, civic engagement, and participation are seamlessly negotiated and redefined across highly personalized networks spanning the spaces of Facebook, Yu-Gi-Oh! and YouTube, today's kids are crafting learning identities—hybrid identities—for themselves that seemingly reject previously distinct modes of being. Writer, designer, reader, producer, teacher, student, gamer—all modes hold equal weight. We used to call this generation "players-producers," "prosumers," or even "multitaskers"; now we just call them *kids*. The phrase that best explains this change comes from Mikey, a student, who in talking about games said, "It's what we do." The "we" he was referring to are kids these days, the young people of his generation.

Parlaying what is known tacitly and explicitly, informally and formally, about how learning happens and deepens, Q2L grounds itself in both the theoretical and the practical educational innovations borne out of learning research done the past 25 years. These innovations speak especially to learning as a process directly tied to contexts in which learners immerse themselves and take on the behaviors and identities endemic to particular domains of knowledge. Gaming and learning scholars have shown that games create for players the kinds of domain-immersive experiences that resemble the most contemporary understandings about learning. To be sure, current learning theories are at odds with education policies and practices interested only in further institutionalizing cognitive theoretical practices, such as rigid assessment programs, which have led increasingly to curricula driven by test-preparatory frameworks. To integrate what is currently known about learning, Q2L is working closely with learning researchers and game designers to create the kinds of immersive and social learning environments that not only facilitate learning, but feature cultural learning spaces that youth currently populate predominantly outside of places called school.

Theoretical and Research Foundations

The work of various fields in education and game design frame the Q2L learning paradigm (Torres 2009). Most significant, the field known as *learning sciences* in the past two decades has made significant scientific contributions to the nature of learning. Researchers in the learning sciences have conducted extensive research that posits learning *as context-based processes mediated by social experiences and technological tools* (Lave 1990; Sawyer 2006). This notion of learning departs from current cognitive theoretical views, which pose that learning and knowledge are computed and stored in the minds of individuals, much like in a computer. These views manifest themselves in prevailing instructional strategies, which take their cues from computer-like learning constructs such as memory, storage, and retrieval (Anderson, Reder, and Simon 1996; Driscoll 2005). Research studies, for example, have shown that the most common teaching strategy in American high schools is initiation/response/evaluation (Christoph and Nystrand 2001), which asks students low-level inferential questions concerned with attaining the right answer. Current national-assessment trends also reflect an adoption of information processing, with the core of the No Child Left Behind Act (2001) serving as an accountability system that assumes that knowledge and knowing can be stored in the mind and appropriately captured through standardized measures.

Situated Learning

In using current learning sciences research, Q2L adopts the view that learning is a highly social endeavor mediated by contexts and the situated practices that occur within particular domains (Brown, Collins, and Duguid 1991; Torres 2009). This view of learning as situated emerges in part out of the notion of *communities of practice*. Jean Lave and Etienne Wenger (1991) define communities of practice as those we participate in throughout our lives. These localities in which practices are exercised and learned *over time* are diverse and include domains such as families, a discipline such as biology, or a sport such as hockey. Distinct to this view of learning is that in addition to the skills and knowledge acquired as a result of participating in such communities, the communities' particular cultural and social practices are also part of what is learned (Klopfer 2008). In this way, a situated-learning view stipulates that learning cannot be computed solely in the head but rather is realized as a result of the interactivity of a dynamic system. These systems construct paradigms in which meaning is produced as a result of humans' social nature and their relationships with the material world of symbols, culture, and historical elements. The structures, then, that define situated learning and inquiry are concerned with the interactivity of these elements, not with systems in the individual mind, such as is proposed in the theory of information processing with stages of memory, storage and retrieval of information, pattern recognition, encoding, and the like (Driscoll 2005). For Q2L, taking the interactivity approach means that learning domains, their respective contexts, and the assessment tools that students and their teachers use to decompose and make meaning are carefully designed to ensure that students engage in situated and authentic, real-world learning experiences.

Much of the work of the learning sciences has been driven by the explicit innovation of learning environments—namely, an understanding of the ecology of learning. Extensive research into the practices of professionals, particularly within the science and math disciplines, has led learning sciences scholars to design effective learning interventions. Much of this work contributed to the now seminal book *How People Learn: Brain, Mind, Experience, and School* (Bransford, Brown, and Cocking 2000) published by the National Research Council. Overall, major contributing disciplines to the learning sciences, as a diverse and interdisciplinary research and education design field, include cognitive science, computer science, psychology, education, neuroscience, and social science. For an overview of the learning sciences, see the introduction to *The Cambridge Handbook of the Learning Sciences* (Sawyer 2006).

Games and learning research, along with studies that report on youths' increasing use of digital media technologies (Jenkins, Clinton, Purushotma, et al. 2006; Lenhardt and Madden 2005; Roberts, Foehr, and Rideout 2005), has led government agencies such as the National Science Foundation and private foundations such as Spencer, Robert Woods Johnson, and MacArthur to fund further research into the potential of games, digital media, and simulations as learning spaces. Indeed, one such project, funded in part by the MacArthur Foundation, is for the design and development of Q2L.

Games and Learning Research

Anchored in the learning sciences, a new field around video games and learning has emerged in recent years. Building on the premise that learning is an immersive process mediated by social activity and technological tools, games and learning researchers have begun to show how the design of video games imbed effective learning principles in highly motivating contexts (Torres 2009). For example, in working with low-income African American students engaged in playing *Civilization III*, both in a high school and in an after-school setting, Kurt Squire (2004) found that the participants, especially those reported to be among the lowest performing, "developed new vocabularies, better understandings of geography, and more robust concepts of world history." *Civilization III* is a highly complex computer strategy game in which its players succeed by building empires—through a *recursive* process of trial and error—by way of managing resources, employing diplomatic and trading skills, and managing the advancement of culture and military power. The participants' teachers had identified them as underachieving in history classes or otherwise disinterested in historical subject matter, yet these kids were able to engage in a game that asked them to account for a host of interacting variables, including, among others, the implications of working within six types of civilizations (e.g., American, Aztec, Iroquois, Zulu), six types government (e.g., despotism, anarchy, communism, democracy), and 13 geographical terrains (jungle, tundra, grasslands, flood plains, and so on). Squire reports elsewhere that engagement in this history-based game simulation motivated some participants to ask questions such as, "Why is it that Europeans colonized the Americas, and why did Africans and Asians not colonize America or Europe?" (Squire 2006, 21)—questions, to be sure, that rarely surface in U.S. history textbooks, which tend to narrativize U.S. and European history as the great westward expansion (Wertsch 1998). Squire's research, like that of others in this new field, points to how the very design attributes of video games support learning (see, e.g., Squire 2004).

Research Precedents

Like Squire's research, Eric Klopfer's work using mobile devices such as handheld computers and mobile phones points to the potential of games as effective learning platforms. As part of MIT's Education Arcade, Klopfer and his colleagues designed a game called *Environmental Detectives*: undergraduates took on the role of environmental engineers to investigate and advise the university about a course to take regarding a pollutant in the groundwater resulting from a recent building construction on campus. The students were given handheld computers programmed with global positioning system software (which allowed them to see their current location as they moved around campus), a schematic map of the area, and "virtual experts" who offered scaffolded information as needed. This project attempted to respond to the difficulty that engineers-in-training have with developing the ability to navigate effectively between primary (quantitative) data and secondary data (such as interviews with witnesses and experts). Hence, a primary goal of this game was to offer players realistic and situated experiences with the challenges of conducting environmental investigations—challenges that require complex thinking in search of dimensional and not "correct" answers, but rather "reasonable explanations." One player in this game reported that it was "a great way to simulate . . . a real life experience. Being in the field enables you to get a much better sense of the terrain that you are working with, and it allows for more authentic feel" (Klopfer 2008, 100). Indeed a core goal of games facilitated by mobile devices is to enable players to engage in complex quests that require interaction with real-world settings and people—from testing pollutants in a water source to interviewing members of the United Nations to sending feedback or information to other players networked into the game.

Systems Thinking

The term *system* is a very broad concept that relates to a number of general areas including social systems, technological systems, and natural systems. Though the subject has been studied from different angles and points of interest, an all-encompassing definition may include the following elements (Assaraf and Orion 2005): a system is an entity designed by humans or by nature that maintains its existence and functions as a whole through the dynamic interaction of its parts. The group of interacting or interdependent parts form a unified whole and are driven by a purpose. Systems attempt to maintain their stability through *feedback*. Hence, the interrelationships among variables are connected by a feedback loop, and the status or behavior of one or more variables consequently affects the status of the other variables (Torres 2009). Systems thinking has been identified as a skill necessary in the twenty-first century (Federation of American Scientists 2006). Researchers, game-development executives, and education leaders at the 2006 Summit on Educational Games—a national conference convened by the Federation of American Scientists, the Entertainment Software Association, and the National Science Foundation—described video games as "able to teach higher-order thinking skills such as strategic thinking, interpretative analysis, problem solving, plan formulation and execution, and adaptation to rapid change" (Federation of American Scientists 2006, 3). In addition, they point out that video games are the medium of attention for youth, who spend on average 50 minutes playing them each day (Roberts, Foehr, and Rideout 2005). While playing video games, young people perform complex tasks within rich and highly immersive multimedia-driven, interactive environments. Such tasks include running political campaigns (*Political Machine*) or football franchises (*NCAA Football 08*), building environmentally sensitive communities (*SimCity*), navigating virtual worlds they create (*Second Life*), managing complex social relationships (*The Sims 2*), or trying to find a diplomatic solution to the Israeli–Palestinian conflict (*Peace-Maker*). Don Menn (1993) claims that students can remember only 10 percent of what they read; 20 percent of what they hear; 30 percent of what they both see and hear if they see visuals related to what they are hearing; 50 percent if they watch someone model something while explaining it; but almost 90 percent if they engage in the job themselves, even if only as a simulation.

Redefining Critical Thinking

Q2L poses that systemic-design thinking defines "criticality" or "critical" thinking. Indeed, current research on video games focuses on the ability to develop a sense of criticality—in other words, the skill of critical thinking. Using the structure of games as a primary framework, Q2L students will be able to design, understand, critique, and manipulate the internal architecture of systems. James Gee (2003, 2007) uses the notion of "semiotic domains" to frame this sort of critical meaning making that learners should be able to do with respect to systems. Approaching meaning making, then, from the linguistics standpoint of semiotics, Gee contends that such an endeavor is characterized by the dynamic interaction between words, symbols, images, and artifacts and human behaviors, affinities and networks. These interactions happen within domains of knowledge to create particular meanings. A domain serves as a locality that draws a type of confinement to a particular space or field. Knowledge domains, which are systems themselves, are as varied as a school, a family, the sport of soccer, or the disciplines of biology and computer science. Each houses characteristics that situate a discourse and particular ways of being and seeing the world. Meaning making, then, is reliant on this *interactionism*. Hence, critical learners must see and appreciate a domain or system as a designed space—"*internally* as a system of interrelated elements making up the possible content of the domain and *externally* as ways of thinking, acting, interacting, and valuing that constitute identities of those people who are members of the affinity group associated with the domain." "It is my contention," Gee claims, "that active, critical learning in any domain should lead to learners becoming, in a sense, *designers*." Critical thinking, as he sees it, "involves learning to think of semiotic domains as design spaces that manipulate us in certain ways . . . and that we can manipulate in certain ways" (2003, 40, 99, 43, emphasis in original). Systemic-design thinking or critical meaning making, then, involves understanding design in two senses: "design" in the morphological sense of form and function, such as the design that "is" a building or a bird, for instance; and "design" in the sociological sense of the interactive, willed, human processes we undertake to meet goals, communicate, and live. Truly understanding the design of domains and systems, then means understanding both structure and human agency.

Reframing Literacy

The push to reframe twenty-first-century education came perhaps most notably from the New London Group (1996) in its manifesto on new literacies in particular and on teaching and learning in general. Made up of international literacy scholars, this group proposed a plan for the future of teaching and learning that called for a pedagogy that was resolute in teaching for critical understanding—by which they meant "conscious awareness and control over the intra-systematic relations of a system" (1996, 85). For this reason, they advocated that "design thinking" drive the creation and methods of postprogressive curricula and pedagogy. Humans design complex systems that interact with designed and natural systems in complex ways. Policy decisions and civic participation in the modern world need to rely on "design thinking" that focuses on intra- and intersystem relationships and patterns as well as on the intended and unintended consequences of local actions within a complex system (witness the intersections of religion, culture, language, industry, economy, and politics in the Iraq War and the disaster to which simplistic linear thinking has led). The New London Group also stressed the importance of seeing language and literacy not just as systems that humans accept and passively use, but as systems that they design in practice moment by moment through decisions and choices and based on deep understanding of the communicative resources (the "design grammar") constituted by different styles of language.

Situating Assessment

The material included in this chapter offers a broad outline for an eventual detailed assessment plan integrated within the sample curriculum. Through work with assessment experts such as Dan Schwartz of Stanford as well as master teachers who will join the team over time, we are refining this framework and toolset of strategies for assessment.

At Q2L, assessment is situated in learning—located in the discourse, actions, and transactions of individuals, peers, and groups. Assessment is a tool for gathering evidence about a student's domain-specific knowledge (concepts and processes), and dispositions). Q2L's Integrated Domains are uniquely designed, life-situated, cross-disciplinary, standards-based resources for its Mission–Quest curriculum. A quick look at the Mission–Quest template (in "Curriculum Structure") provides a schema for the embedded choreography of situated Q2L learning and its assessment—namely, its focus on data-collection and data-analysis tools to evaluate contexts of knowing: what, how, when.

The following key principles and values guide Q2L teachers' work around assessment:

1. Assessment is situated in learning—located in the discourse, actions, and transactions of individuals, peers, and groups. Embedded assessment assumes that data-collection and data-analysis tools will be appropriately chosen on a trajectory of activity:
- Planning Quests
- Doing Quests
- Culminating Quests
- Culminating Discovery Mission Fluency Assessment
- Culminating Boss-Level Fluency Assessment
- Teacher's reflection on Mission–Quest results.

2. An assessment program should be designed to allow learners to assess themselves eventually.

3. Assessments should measure the extent to which students can innovate within a domain.

4. Understanding students' learning and the school's effectiveness is best facilitated by data.

5. "Smartools" are a primary form of assessment. Students use data provided by Smartools that they themselves create to understand and meet their own learning goals.

6. Students are accountable to themselves, to their peer community, and to the school.

7. Success is mediated by continual reflection and evaluation of the school's goals and mission.

8. Knowledge to be assessed emerges from engaged participation, reasoning, and resolution of Missions and their Quests.

9. Assessment tools support valid inferences about learning. Assessment tools must facilitate answers to the question: "What does a particular performance reveal about how students know and about how they reason with and use their knowledge?"

10. Assessment is dynamic: equitable and inclusive, it meets student needs before, during, after, and in between learning experiences (Delandshere 2002). Planning and student advisory structures exist to design, monitor, counsel, or adjust learning Quests to meet students' learning trajectory needs. The major challenges of this standard are finding out what all students do know and creating a learning environment with "no floor, no ceiling" so that they all can work toward their maximum potential, achievement, and sense of self-worth.

11. Participatory assessment requires that expectations, co-constructed and delivered criteria, and documentation be "open source" for all participants. Students need to know what is

expected, specifically how they can successfully complete Missions and their correlated Quests. Supporting this goal will be students' coparticipation in choosing learning activities and eventually in designing Quests, constant reflection, and advisory structures. Processes such as purposeful collection of data, theorizing, reasoning, and critical reflection skills are pivotal for knowledge seeking, and performance is assessed using holistic, qualitative techniques. Thus, students need to be involved in setting criteria for assessment and using these criteria as a means to their own ends or aim.

Toolkits

Assessment resource Toolkits support teachers' dynamic assessment of student learning. Principles, guidelines, templates, and exemplars are included in Toolkits for making assessments at formative and summative stages of Missions and their correlated Quests:

- Rubrics (holistic and analytic templates: *concepts, processes, and dispositions*)
- Observation protocols (varying formats and suggestions to capture data):
   In situ events
   Students' learning logs/journals
   Prior knowledge for planning Missions and Quests
   Interventions
- Questioning protocols:
   Teacher's instructional-design questions
   Teacher's questioning of students as scaffolding strategy

Students' questioning ("What needs discovery?" "What is known?"
"What do I need to find out?")
Students' metacognitive strategies and reflection (In Being Me formats or Think Alouds)
- Interview protocols (teacher–student; peer–peer; student–expert)
- Interpretative representations criteria:
  Writing (all forms)
  Mapping (diagrams, schematics)
  Drawing
  Performing or presenting (live and online)
- Dedicated instructional-assessment methods
  Reciprocal teaching
  Guided prompting
- Discourse analysis (teacher–student talk; peer talk)
- Games as assessment: scenarios demonstrating uses of games as assessment systems.

Research design for gathering qualitative and quantitative data on student achievement over time can be developed with domain-specific educational research experts.

In sum, Q2L learning and its assessment cohabit the culture and context of its game-based, systemic design. How students know is embodied in what they do. How teachers come to know how students are doing is embodied in a cyclic layering of assessment activity: (1) collecting data, (2) interpreting data, and (3) documenting data. "Curriculum and Instruction" includes Mission curriculum templates indicating how we think Q2L participants can engage in a continuum of knowledge questing.

Three Learning Dimensions

Three learning dimensions frame the curriculum and assessment program at Q2L:

- Dimension One: Civic/Social-Emotional Learning
- Dimension Two: Design
- Dimension Three: Content

For each of the learning dimensions, rubrics assess specific competencies (see table 1). Competencies and the learning principles they represent come from Q2L values, as expressed in this planning document. They include:

1. *Learning for Well-Being and Emotional Intelligence* At Q2L, various programs compose a Wellness domain, such as an online social-networking platform, Being Me, and Home Base advisories. The Wellness domain supports students' emotional, nutritional, and physical development. A unique aspect of our programming is guided by the understanding that emotions are deeply connected to learning. Hence, opportunities are provided for students to understand and reflect on emotions.

2. *Learning for Design and Innovation* Q2L's standards-based curriculum supports students in becoming active problem solvers and innovators of the twenty-first century. Tinkering and theory building are critical practices supported across the curriculum. Students are given time, space, and purpose to tinker with systems (games, simulations, small machines, etc.). Students tinker and theorize as a core method of discovery.

3. *Learning for Complexity (Systemic Reasoning)*   A core goal of our pedagogy is to help students learn to reason about their world. Systemic reasoning, or the ability to see the world in terms of the many interrelated systems that make it up—from biological to political to technological and social—supports students in meeting this goal.

4. *Learning for Critical Thinking, Judgment, and Credibility*   One core component of our learning model is helping young people to understand many of the unintended consequences that may arise as part of their participation with and use of digital media. Students will learn how to judge the credibility of information drawn from online resources, for example, and learn how to reason about and evaluate content. They will learn how to manage and synthesize multiple streams of information. They will learn to be critical thinkers who are able to appreciate, debate, and negotiate different points of view. Most important, our curriculum focuses on equipping students with an understanding of new models of citizenship, civic participation, and public participation made possible within today's networked learning landscape.

5. *Learning Using a Design Methodology*   Our curriculum creates contexts for ongoing feedback and reflection. This approach creates opportunities for students to demonstrate and share their knowledge with teachers and peers. Across the curriculum, students act as sociotechnical engineers in the creation of playful systems—games, models, simulations, stories, and so on. Through *designing play*, students learn to think analytically and holistically, to experiment and test out theories, and to consider other people as part of the systems they create and inhabit. Game design serves as the pedagogy underlying this work.

6. *Learning with Technology and Smart Tools* Within our curriculum, students learn how to build Smartools, or "tools to
think with," such as maps, online dictionaries, equations, and
computer simulations, to name but a few. Through these tools,
students have access to continual and transparent feedback on
achievement toward learning objectives.

Table 1
Three Competency Dimensions

DIMENSION ONE Civic and Social-Emotional Learning	DIMENSION TWO Design	DIMENSION THREE Content
Apply across All Domains	Apply across All Domains	Knowledge Domain content aligns with New York state standards
• Teaming, learning from peers and others;	• Systemic thinking	• The Way Things Work
• Planning, organizing, adapting, and managing goals and priorities;	• Digital media tool use	• Being, Space, and Place
• Reflecting and self-assessing in action and on action;	• Iteration	• Codeworlds
• Persisting to overcome complex challenges;	• Representation	• Sports for the Mind
• Attending to diverse and global perspectives; using the world as a learning space;	• Communication	• Wellness
• Behaving ethically and responsibly;	• Intelligent resourcing for new ideas	

Table 1
(continued)

DIMENSION ONE Civic and Social-Emotional Learning	DIMENSION TWO Design	DIMENSION THREE Content
Apply across All Domains	Apply across All Domains	Knowledge Domain content aligns with New York state standards
▪ Caring about others, developing positive relationships	▪ Designing play	▪ Mission Lab
▪ Recognizing and managing emotions	▪ Designing for innovation	▪ Being Me
	▪ Participating in interest-driven communities	▪ Home Base
		▪ All other nodes

Curriculum and Instruction

At the center of Q2L is an approach to pedagogy that connects game design and systems thinking across a standards-based curriculum. This pedagogy includes a reforming of traditional disciplines into Integrated Domains, informed by a core set of learning practices.

Pedagogy

Q2L is a dynamic learning system composed of a set of inter-related parts, from key practices and learning strategies to core resources, personnel, and space. At the heart of the system is a curriculum that interweaves state standards with ways of knowing and doing. The curriculum is delivered and supported by an innovative instructional model that fosters student problem solving, interdisciplinary learning, collaborative student work, reflective practices, and high levels of student engagement and ownership in the learning process. Students are provided with multiple learning contexts for engaging in gamelike learning, contexts in which students receive immediate feedback on progress, have access to tools for planning and reflection, and are given opportunities for mastery of specialist language and practices.

Here we present a set of key values and principles guiding Q2L's curriculum, instruction, and assessment plan.

Core Values

Pedagogy

1. A sustainable world requires that twenty-first-century learners have the capacity to design innovations.
2. The use of new media and social media technologies, including games, not only engages students but holds the potential for students to make changes to their own lives and communities.
3. Systemic reasoning, peer learning, creativity, and civic participation are vital twenty-first-century competencies.
4. Student identity as learner, mentor, and citizen should be recognized and supported as constantly evolving.
5. Provocative, essential questions guide student learning and provide students with the opportunity to ask more precise questions and thereby discover answers for themselves.
6. Design, inquiry, argumentation, and analysis play a central role in students' endeavors in developmentally appropriate ways.
7. Students respond to a need to know and are motivated to ask hard questions, to look for complex answers, and to take on the responsibility of imagining solutions with others.
8. Missions and Quests are tools for building bridges between bodies of knowledge and what a child learns in school, on the one hand, and his or her life outside the classroom, on the other.

9. The approach to learning and assessment is based on social-cultural principles (versus behaviorist or cognitivist principles) that see learning as a result of the interactions among people (novices and experts), technologies, knowledge, behaviors, beliefs, symbols, rules, culture, and space.

10. Spaces for play and experimentation are critical to the cultivation of creativity and innovation.

11. Students are given time, space, and purpose to tinker with systems.

12. Iteration and prototyping: students work through multiple versions of any idea or solution, integrating ongoing feedback into the learning process and developing debriefings that identify strengths and weaknesses of both process and solution.

13. Peer education is an important part of the curriculum; students share their own interests and expertise with each other.

14. Students act as sociotechnical engineers in the creation of playful systems—games, models, simulations, and stories. Through designing play, students learn to think analytically and holistically, to experiment and test out theories, and to consider other people as part of the systems they create and inhabit. Game design serves as the pedagogy underlying this work.

15. Writing occurs across the curriculum, with students engaging in reading and writing daily in a range of forms and contexts—some analytical, some expressive, some descriptive or creative.

Learning

1. Real learning is participatory and experiential. Students learn by proposing, testing, playing with, and validating theories about the world.

2. Learning takes place across a range of learning communities where student expertise and interests are valued.
3. School is a context to activate and create coherence across learning communities.
4. Learning begins with identification to the social norms and conventions of a domain. Learning is inert without this identification.
5. Students should have a variety of meaningful membership experiences in "pro-amateur" communities.
6. Students should be provided with multiple learning contexts for engaging in gamelike learning—contexts in which they receive immediate feedback on progress, have access to tools for planning and reflection, and are given opportunities for mastery of specialist language and practices.
7. Mathematical processes, methods, and strategies are integrated throughout the curriculum, supported through rigorous work with manipulatives, models, and simulations.

Assessment

1. Assessment is situated in learning—located in the discourse, actions, and transactions of individuals, peers, and groups (Salvia, J., and J. Ysseldyke. 2007).
2. The assessment program is designed to allow learners to assess themselves eventually.
3. Assessments measure the extent to which students can innovate within a domain.
4. Understanding students' learning and the school's effectiveness is best facilitated by data.
5. Smartools are a primary form of assessment: students use data provided by Smartools they themselves create to understand and meet their own learning goals.

6. Students are accountable to themselves, to their peer community, and to the school.

7. Success is mediated by continual reflection and evaluation of the school's goals and mission.

8. Knowledge to be assessed emerges from engaged participation, reasoning, and resolution of Missions and their Quests.

9. Assessment tools support valid inferences about learning. Assessment tools must facilitate answers to the question: "What does a particular performance reveal about how students know and about how they reason with and use their knowledge?"

10. Assessment is dynamic, equitable, and inclusive, meeting student needs before, during, after, and in between learning experiences.

11. Participatory assessment requires that expectations, co-constructed and delivered criteria, and documentation be "open source" for all participants.

School Culture

1. Attention to well-being and social-emotional learning is as important as attention to academic learning.

2. Equity and social justice drive all aspects of the school.

3. School governance systems are inclusive of all stakeholder voices.

4. All members of the Q2L community hold high expectations for all students.

5. School is a practice space where the life systems that students inhabit and share with others are modeled, designed, taken apart, and reengineered as a strategy for learning.

6. Students play games and reflect on their learning within them.

7. Games are not only models for helping students think about how the world works, but also a dynamic medium through which to engage socially and to develop a deeper understanding of their place in the world.

8. All members of the Q2L community are encouraged to take risks, make meaning, and act creatively and resourcefully.

Domains

1. Each domain is concerned with helping students develop a game design and systems perspective of the world, by which we mean students learn how to see and understand the world from the perspective of the dynamic relationships between parts of a whole.

2. Domains allow students to explore diverse modes of accumulating, creating, understanding, and using knowledge.

3. Domains foster the targeted assimilation and synthesis of data, theories, and hypotheses of traditional academic disciplines and develop habits of mind through which a student's thoughts and actions demonstrate progressive understanding and personal growth.

4. Domains are defined by a set of socially acceptable norms, values, knowledge, and ways of validating and creating knowledge.

5. Domains are also defined by clear trajectories toward mastery, although these trajectories are often varied.

6. Domains offer opportunities for students to consider and design structured, physical models of complex problems.

Systems and Design Core Mechanics (Competencies)

The systems and design core mechanics are recursive in nature in that they are continually reviewed throughout the academic year and are applied to all domains. They include

- Distinguishing what is important and salient.
- Identifying causal relationships among things and ideas.
- Sequencing causes and effects to act and think effectively over time.
- Establishing patterns and relationships over time and space.
- Clarifying disparate bits of information and reconciling them to a larger whole.
- Resolving tensions and discrepancies within existing structures.
- Explaining knowledge in terms relative to the individual whose discourse is the reference point.
- Providing relevant examples from other knowledge bases that help to demonstrate and exemplify the efficacy of primary knowledge.
- Applying knowledge to new circumstances and situations.
- Justifying a theory or idea by offering evidence in its defense or designing and conducting an experiment to test the idea.
- Comparing and contrasting current knowledge with other knowledge of a similar kind to establish constraints.
- Synthesizing information so that the sum of knowledge is greater than its parts.
- Iterating to solve problems.

Key Learning Practices

Five key practices are emphasized in all aspects of Q2L:
1. *Systems Thinking*   Video games, early research suggests, are well suited to encouraging fluency in specialist language, literacy skills, and "meta-level reflection on the skills and processes that designer-players use in building . . . systems" (Gee 2007, 15). A principal intent of Q2L is to provide students with ways of

knowing related to the design and analysis of systems, be they games or civilizations. The development of *systemic-design thinking* is a core skill that Q2L students will continually develop throughout their tenure and will help them practice

a. Understanding feedback dynamics (i.e., reinforcing and balancing feedback loops): that microlevel changes can affect macrolevel processes.

b. Understanding system dynamics: that multiple (i.e., dynamic) relationships exist within a system.

c. Understanding hidden dimensions of a system: that modifications to system elements can lead to changes that are not easily recognizable within a system.

d. Understanding the quality of relationships within a system: that a system is working or not working at optimal levels.

e. Understanding homologies: that similar system dynamics can exist in other systems that may appear to be entirely different.

2. *Play Design*   Students act as sociotechnical engineers in the creation of playful systems—games, models, simulations, and stories. Students learn about the way systems work and how they can be modified or changed. Through designing play, they learn to think analytically and holistically, to experiment and test out theories, and to consider other people as part of the systems they create and inhabit. Game design serves as the pedagogy underlying this work.

3. *Intelligent Resourcing*   Students gain the ability to find and use resources on demand, with intelligence, judgment, and sophistication through immersion in challenging, collaborative

learning experiences. Peer education is an important part of the curriculum—students sharing their own interests and expertise with each other.

4. *Meaning Production* Students learn how to produce meaning —for themselves and for external audiences—within complex, multimodal contexts. Creativity, expression, and innovation underlies this learning as students practice producing meaning through the coding and decoding of linguistic, numeric, social, and cultural systems. This approach challenges traditional barriers between consumer and producer/viewer and designer, allowing students to gain the skills to act as full citizens within a networked, participatory landscape.

5. *Tinkering* Students are given time, space, and purpose to tinker with systems (games, simulations, small machines, social systems, ecologies, etc.). By making small-scale alterations in both experimental and directed ways, students reveal the system's underlying model. Breaking down systems in order to discover new ways of acting within them is a core component of this approach. Students tinker as a core method of discovery.

Key Learning Strategies

1. Creating a Need to Know
One of Q2L's learning goals is to create in students a *need to know*. This means creating learning environments that support situated inquiry and discovery so that students have rich contexts within which to integrate concepts and content. Creating a need to know encourages students to persist in solving a problem, to create theories, to test out those theories, evaluate

outcomes, ask "what if," and try again. It creates conditions for an exchange of questions and expertise across a community of learners working on similar problems and leads to a natural engagement with learning about the issue at hand. Students learn to connect engagement and interest with the need to plan, a need to know exactly what they are trying to figure out. As a result, students learn how to ask good questions and seek out the resources (be they technological, social, or academic) that will lead them to answers.

2. Writing across the Curriculum

Rather than seeing writing as an activity related only to traditional domains of ELA and social studies, Q2L instead uses writing across the curriculum. Students engage in reading and writing daily in a range of forms and contexts, some analytical, some expressive, some descriptive or creative. Text and media-based platforms allow students to use writing to "think with," and extra attention is paid to ensuring that students gain the reading and comprehension skills necessary for student achievement.

3. Foundations in Math

Because of the importance of numeracy and mathematical thinking, Q2L's curriculum builds on a rigorous sequence in mathematics, which underlies work in each of the school's six learning contexts. Mathematical processes, methods, and strategies are integrated throughout the curriculum, supported through rigorous work with manipulatives, models, and simulations.

4. Iteration and Prototyping

Curricular experiences within Q2L are based on a process of prototyping and iteration, based on a game design methodology: students work through multiple versions of any idea or solution, integrating ongoing feedback into the learning process and developing debriefings that identify strengths and weaknesses of both process and solution. In some cases, students may choose to build on other students' previous solutions or approaches, seeing themselves as contributors to a larger body of collaboratively generated knowledge. Participants in Q2L build both cultural and intellectual capital as a result. Students are encouraged to manage and reflect on their evolving identities as learners, producers, peers, researchers, and citizens.

5. Special Learning Environments

Q2L students have the opportunity to work with several digitally based learning environments through the support offered by its founding partner, the Institute of Play. These environments are integrated into the overall Q2L curriculum and are used by students throughout the year in Home Base and domain classes.

SMALLab   Students have a chance to work in a special learning space called SMALLab, run by the Institute of Play and Parsons. SMALLab is a mixed-reality environment that uses motion-capture cameras and top-down digital projection to create learning scenarios that students interact with around targeted content chosen by teachers. Students use wireless controllers to interact with digital objects projected on the floor. This form of interaction with content and concepts supports a form of embodied learning in which kids learn in kinesthetic ways. Since its inception, SMALLab has been tested with kids and their teachers as they work with math, science, and ELA content. Support for SMALLab is provided through Intel Research (http://smallab.parsons.edu).

Mission Lab   Mission Lab is Q2L's curriculum development studio located inside the school and staffed by the Institute of Play. It is a support space for teachers and contains resources that can be used by students as part of their curriculum work, including access to game designers with expertise in the design of learning environments. Mission Lab represents a new model of an institution that we feel is critical to supporting pedagogical models emerging from within MacArthur's Digital Media

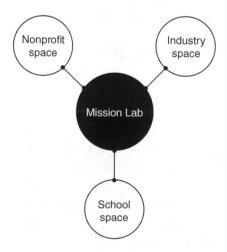

and Learning initiative. This type of institution acts a bridging "node" within a broader learning network, connecting and synthesizing expertise and resources from school institutions, nonprofit organizations and foundations, and industry.

Mission Lab has been built into the design of the school in such a way as to be integral to its learning model. The school has thus been freed to define itself as one node within a larger network of nodes supporting student learning. The lab has four primary responsibilities:

1. Support current and future curriculum development through collaboration with Quest teachers and content experts.
2. Offer professional development for current and incoming teachers.
3. Design learning tools and Toolkits for use in the school and within the DML network.
4. Undertake research and development around assessment and student development.

Being Me   Being Me is a closed social-network platform that has been custom designed for the school and is to be used by students throughout the day. The platform allows students to post work, create a blog, form discussion groups, tag resources for use in their classes, track their mood, find collaborators, and much more. Only members of the Q2L learning community have access to the site, so it is a safe online space that students can be use to extend their own learning. The development of Being Me was funded by the Robert Wood Johnson Foundation pioneer portfolio and designed by the Institute of Play.

Essential Design Principles of Being Me
- Layering of access to work produced (friendlocking profiles and access to other forms of shared content)
- Specialization (in contrast to standardization): multiple forms of expertise exist across the network
- Competition and status
- Sharing and recommending
- Reviewing and sharing of feedback as a form of assessment
- Appreciation and validation (a celebration of what one knows and does)
- Production of collective, external artifacts
- Distribution of expertise and knowledge across the community of practice

Being Me as Student-Driven Wellness Program   Unique in its emphasis on creating opportunities for learning within a game-inspired curriculum, the school is committed to linking students' physical, social, and emotional wellness within an overall ecology of learning. Being Me is a learning tool at the heart of Q2L's mission. Combining a game-based wellness curriculum with an online social-networking site that supports youth-led activity, Being Me supports the Q2L mission of student agency and identity formation, serving as a platform to engage students in connecting out-of-school and in-school experiences in ways that help them think about their health in multidimensional terms. What issues do students consider important, worrisome, private, or confusing? How do they choose to express their interests and concerns? What ecologies of resources do they create, share, and seek out?

Being Me as Healthy Identity Development   Being Me takes its mission of a unified approach seriously: to build on the digitally diverse lives of young people to create learners like no others—self-aware, healthful, engaged, powerful citizens of a sustainable world. Being Me's online presence—a social-network site where students can document, discover, explore, "take on," and play with a broad range of ideas related to health and wellness, create and share media, post comments, create groups, share and find expertise, seek mentorship in issues they need help with—is a central social and data hub in the school. Its physical presence—a series of "wellness Quests" integrated across the curriculum that respond to this online activity—forms one of the school's cultural cores.

Being Me supports the belief that students must practice and play to be able to enact sustainable and healthful identities. The more spaces, communities, and contexts that they gain experience in as practitioners of reflective learning about their own lives, the healthier they and their communities grow. Within the spaces of Being Me, students "learn to be," taking on identities as mathematicians, scientists, medical detectives, diplomats, healers, writers, historians, and teenagers as they work through a challenge-based wellness curriculum that has questing to learn at its core. Two key literacies of the twenty-first century—game design and systems thinking—support students in this work, giving rise to new understandings and strategies for approaching health and wellness concerns.

Being Me as Multifaceted Tool   As a learning tool, Being Me provides opportunities for students to increase their understanding of issues they identify as important within an environment that supports opportunities for interaction and feedback. (Eighty-one percent of those who drop out of school claim that "opportunities for real world learning" would have improved their chances of staying in school [Bridgeland, DiIulio, and Morison 2006, 9].) As a curricular tool, Being Me includes attention to situating the students' personal health and wellness within larger systems of influence, including peer groups, family, community, and society more generally. As a data repository, Being Me captures the interests and concerns of youth via the materials they make and share, the conversations and debates they engage in, the people they reach out to, and the communities they create. Data generated by students in both the online network and wellness Quests can be used as powerful tools to support future decision making and to adapt academic and support systems to individual needs. Finally, as a networking space, Being Me offers students a chance to participate within a range of peer groups in public and private settings, defined and managed by the students themselves. Through Being Me, Q2L youth are virtually able to invent their own wellness curriculum, forged by their own need to express themselves, communicate, and share what they are living with among peers and others in their learning community.

Being Me for Adults   In order for Being Me to be perceived and used by students as a trusted space for sharing and personal expression, teachers must develop and support this capacity. To facilitate this result, we have created a professional development program that trains teachers in all aspects of Being Me. Unlike in typical professional development, which supports teachers in the implementation of pedagogical techniques or curricular tools, in this program teachers are participants in Being Me. They learn experientially while they use the site for their own wellness development. This approach is informed by the ideas of parallel process and family systems theory, both of which illuminate how the student community's wellness is dependent on the adult community's wellness. At Q2L, we know that our adults need to actively foster their own wellness in order to be effective mentors, teachers, and role models.

Integrated Domains: Situated Ways of Knowing

Q2L is made up of five "Integrated Domains": The Way Things Work; Being, Space, and Place; Codeworlds; Wellness; and a

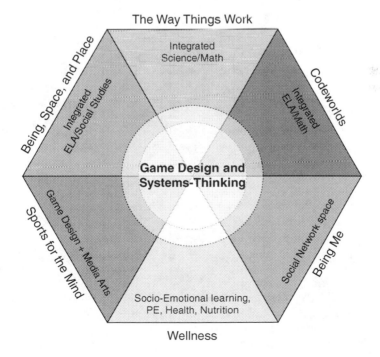

media literacy/design course called Sports for the Mind. These Integrated Domains are interdisciplinary and integrate the traditional domains of math, science, history, and literature to form practice spaces for students to gain experience in different ways of knowing. Each learning context is concerned with helping students develop a game design and systems perspective of the world, by which we mean students learn how to see and understand the world from the perspective of the dynamic relationships between parts of a whole.

This approach to understanding resists customary methods of isolated analytic problem solving, which ask learners to break down problems into component parts for discrete examination outside of consideration of the whole—a skill that is no longer sufficient in today's complex global society. By examining the interrelationships of elements within whole systems via a game design pedagogy, learners are better equipped to recognize patterns that offer critical insights into the nature and complexity of systems (social, technological, natural, and imaginary) shaping their world. Q2L teachers consider what students bring *to* any experience of learning, what they take *from* it, what they do to engage in and progress within their quest *during* the experience itself, and what happens *between* experiences. Curriculum development thus attends equally to the design of phases, passages, and transitions between concepts, framing all curricular development within systemic terms.

The Integrated Domains support work in the master context, *game design and systems*, which organizes all experiences and ways of knowing within the school. The next few sections show the relationships between the domains.

The Way Things Work

Students practice taking different kinds of systems apart and modifying, remixing, and inventing systems of their own. Students learn about system structure and dynamics through hands-on work with concrete applications, such as breaking down small machines in science. Students design systems and make measurements that are relevant to improving the quality of their lives. Through the use of different systems such as games, models, digital simulations, and stories, students learn to engage with their world holistically in order to discover strategies for participating in the world and creating change.

Domain Core Values

- All systems can be taken apart.
- Students gain a particular perspective of the world when they are given opportunities to take apart, modify, and invent systems.
- Twenty-first-century inventions are necessary to a sustainable world.
- Emphasis is on helping students to recognize patterns, identify structure, and formulate general principles.
- Work in this domain should reflect current needs in innovation (e.g., green technologies).
- The Way Things Work supports connective thinking and creativity across physical, social, technological, and cultural systems. Connective thinking and creativity are key literacies of the twenty-first century.
- Creating models of systems is a concrete way to give physical description to complex phenomenon.

Being, Space, and Place

Students consider time, space, and human geographies as forces that shape the development of ideas, expression, and values. In Being, Space, and Place, students are challenged to see themselves in relation to the spatial and social world around them, focusing on the interaction between the individual and the web of systems they influence and inhabit. Students explore personal, sociocultural, physical, living, and imaginary systems as contexts for learning—in the process seeking to understand the nature of the individual and how the identity of that individual shapes their world. Point of view and perspective taking are core tools in this domain; by responding to viewpoints, debating, and taking a stand, students become aware of systems of relationships embodied through empathy, cooperation, reciprocation, ethics, tolerance, and citizenry in a global world.

Domain Core Values
- We travel within multiple cultural systems.
- Humans are agents who can influence the world around them.
- Students mindfully take apart, create, and analyze personal, sociocultural, physical, living, and imaginary systems.
- A person's identity informs the way he or she interacts with the world.
- Understanding and taking on diverse perspectives leads to deeper levels of complex thinking.
- The design of the curriculum offers students opportunities to take a stand on issues they care about while exhibiting empathy, cooperation, reciprocation, ethical standards, and tolerance for diverse points of view.
- Agency is developed out of membership and influenceability within and across communities.

- Learning is anchored within a framework and understanding of what it means to be an active global citizen.
- Students understand and appreciate multiple perspectives when using strategies such as dramatic role play, literature response, and debate.
- The continuous interplay of contextual factors—such as being, space, and place—influences how we experience and make meaning of the web of systems we study and inhabit in our daily lives.

Codeworlds

Students practice decoding, authoring, manipulating, and unlocking meaning in coded worlds in order to meet shared needs or for their own purposes. Work in this learning context requires students to practice with the concept of language and literacy across disciplines, from math to ELA to computer programming. Codeworlds draws on games as learning environments that produce meaning through the interpretation of symbolic codes ordering our world. As students reflect on how the underlying rules of a system shape expression and communication, they gain experience in comprehending the world as a metasystem made up of multiple systems, each containing a set of values, assumptions, and perspectives.

Domain Core Values
- All codes convey meaning.
- Literacy across systems is necessary: code is key to that literacy.
- Math is a language that describes the world.
- Students gain literacy in multiple languages.
- Code is a symbolic system that is predictable, repeatable, and interpretable.

- Code is a material for the representation of ideas.
- Code is a common way of making meaning between people (i.e., it is shared).
- Code is a foundation for innovation.
- Code is organized by rule sets.
- Code is a dynamic system.
- All language is constructed and can evolve and change.
- Ordering, sequencing, patterning are ways of organizing content.
- By manipulating language, one can create worlds.
- Meaning can be translated across code.
- Students reimagine worlds through code.
- Code demonstrates the power of language.

Wellness

At Q2L, Wellness is a domain and schoolwide practice where students appreciate and know what it means to be healthy. Wellness situates personal, social, emotional, and physical health within larger systems, including peer groups, family, community, and society. In sixth-grade Wellness, for example, students learn to see the body as a complex, dynamic system affected and changed by systems that are both internal and external to it. Through practice in the Wellness domain, students develop strategies for keeping their bodies running at optimal physical, social, and emotional levels while learning to make healthy choices. Wellness expertise is distributed across disciplines such as exercise science, human sexuality, personal health, nutrition, youth development, expressive arts, mindfulness, interpersonal and group dynamics, life coaching, conflict mediation, and movement. Q2L students cultivate ownership of wellness practices that have an impact on all interactions in their daily lives and the communities of which they are part.

Domain Core Values
- Integrative health exists across physical, social, and emotional systems.
- Wellness is a strategy by which students can learn to recognize and manage emotions, care about others, make good decisions, behave ethically and responsibly, develop positive relationships, and maintain their community's well-being.
- Students understand and respect self, self and others, and self in community. Q2L values a culture of kindness.
- Wellness is dynamic, emergent, and changing over time.
- With responsibility for and ownership of wellness practice, students gain and sustain lived, "true to you" health.
vHealth reflects energy and balance—equipoised states of being. vMindfulness and reflection support well-being.
- Wellness happens with active, engaged, "can do" participation.
- Wellness philosophy informs the Q2L model of being in a community of learners.
- The Wellness domain supports learning well and learning to be well in mind, feelings, and body.

Sports for the Mind

The fluent use of new media across networks has become an essential prerequisite for a productive career, prosperous life, and civic engagement in the twenty-first century. Sports for the Mind is a primary space of practice attuned to new media literacies, which are multimodal and multicultural, operating as they do within specific contexts for specific purposes. Work in this domain introduces students to tools that are foundational to the curriculum: game design platforms in the sixth grade; programming tools in the seventh grade; tools for working with virtual worlds in the eighth grade; and data-visualization and knowledge-management tools in the ninth. The selection of tool sets is made in coordination with the rest of the curriculum.

Domain Core Values

• Productive and prosperous citizens in the twenty-first century need to possess a fundamental understanding of the various modes of new media communication.
• Students learn and exhibit new media literacies most powerfully when they take on multiple tasks in the creation of new media artifacts.
• Tool sets organize and support specific forms of literacy.
• Game design, media arts, computer programming, and urban design are applied contexts for the acquisition of new media literacies.

Curriculum Structure

Learning at Q2L occurs via an innovative model that situates the acquisition of specific skills and ways of knowing within Discovery Missions, or challenge-based problem sets. This chapter describes the structure and rational behind Discovery Missions, concluding with a curriculum template to be used in support of their design.

Discovery Missions

The Q2L curriculum is delivered through central organizing structures known as Discovery Missions and Boss Levels, which together represent a common organizing principle for games. Students navigate each of the Integrated Domains described in "Curriculum and Instruction" through immersion in complex, interdisciplinary problems that require students to gain standard-based skills and fluencies in order to solve them. In traditional terms, Discovery Missions represent a *unit* of study.

Each 12-week semester is divided into two parts: Discovery Missions, which last 10 weeks; and Boss Levels, which run during the last 2 weeks of a semester, providing a 2-week "intensive." In a Boss Level, students and teachers work collaboratively on a capstone project that integrates ways of knowing experienced within the previous 10 weeks. A Boss Level acts as a kind of a "space of defense"; students draw on an inventory of acquired content, processes, resources, and relationships to overcome a final challenge. During this time, students participate in a rigorous process of research, theory building, hypothesis testing, evaluation, and critique—all followed by a public defense of results. Student-led teacher conferences take place at the end of the semester, allowing students, teachers, and parents/caregivers to review student achievement and progress together.

All Missions are designed to get students to

• Reflect on what they know how to do now and what they need to learn how to do in order to complete the Mission successfully.
• Gather data and manipulate resources.
• Create inferences.
• Theorize and generate solutions.
• Evaluate results.

The Way Things Work	
Being, Space, and Place	synthesizing context
Codeworlds	
Wellness	
Sports for the Mind	
10-week Missions	2-week Boss Level

Quests

Each Discovery Mission is made up of a series of smaller Quests, or goal-oriented challenges that equip students with necessary data, knowledge, resources, and practices to solve the larger Mission. In traditional terms, Quests are like subunits of a larger unit of study.

Quests are designed as active "data expeditions": students collect information and resources of different types (scientific data, writing, statistical or economic data, physical samples, etc.). Students then manipulate, analyze, and shape these data in ways that allow them to gain expertise in the standards defining the knowledge core of each domain. For example, sixth-grade students on a Discovery Mission within Being, Space, and Place may be required to find definitions of key terms hidden with the html of Web pages distributed across the Internet. In completing this Quest, students have to learn the basic syntax of HTML, become fluent in the use of search engines, and learn how to assess the credibility of sources. Once gathered, the key terms form the basis of vocabulary, reading, and comprehension work. The Quests' structure, enabling spiral, and fit to the larger goals of a Discovery Mission provide the vehicle for student self-assessment about "what they need to know" and "how to find out" and for teachers to gather assessment data based on evidence of their achievements in situated contexts.

Missions contain from 4 to 10 Quests, which vary in length and complexity. A Quest is designed for completion either by individuals or by students working in small teams. Students know a Mission's goal before it begins. As the school gains upper grades, part of the curriculum will involve the design of Quests by the older students for the lower grades.

Examples of Things Students Might Do as Part of a Quest
- Analyze 20 Wikipedia pages.
- Go to a local deli to collect pricing information on various fruits and set up Excel spreadsheets to organize the data.
- Work with an online telescope to gather data on star types or positions.
- Send text messages to relatives about family histories.
- Go to a museum to explore the details of an exhibition.
- Talk to experts or their neighbors and record oral histories.
- Read a text and pull out key ideas.
- Take apart a bicycle to locate a key component.
- Use various resources to break a secret code.
- Do a science experiment.

Types of Quests
The following list includes different kinds of Quests that can be used in the design of Discovery Missions. The list will expand over time as further work is done with the Q2L curriculum model.

- *Collect Quest*   Goal is to collect/harvest x resources.
- *Puzzle Quest*   Goal is to solve a problem (might also be called a Code Cracker Quest).
- *Share Quest*   Goal is to share x resources.
- *Drama Quest*   Goal is to enact a system or behavior.
- *Conquest*   Goal is to capture a territory or resource.
- *Grow Quest*   Goal is to increase the number of resources in a system.

- *Shrink Quest* Goal is to decrease the number of resources in a system.
- *Maze Quest* Goal is to find a way through a space (about navigation).
- *Story Quest* Goal is to create a story.
- *Delivery Quest* Goal is to deliver *x* resources.
- *Seek and Destroy Quest* Goal is to eliminate something (e.g., eliminate all misspelled words from a document).
- *Spy or Scout Quest* Goal is to observe and gather information and report back.
- *Research Quest* Research a question and return with the answer. This research might take any number of forms, from questioning friends and teachers for viewpoints to reading books in a virtual library to deciphering runes and hieroglyphs.
- *Design Quest* Goal is to make something to be used in the Quest.
- *Apprentice Quest* Goal is for a player to assume the duties of an expert character in the game after having learned about what this expert does.
- *Tracking Quest* Goal is to track something and report back on its movement or change.
- *Experiment Quest* Goal is to find the results of a scientific experiment.

Structure of Boss Levels

Students within a section organize into teams and create a response to a final challenge. As a section, the students together create a set of criteria to evaluate the teams' outcomes and vote later for a single solution the section wants to put forward for final judging against solutions from other sections. Sections have the opportunity to spend one or two days improving the selected solution before the final judging. Students are selected on a random and rotating basis to sit on the final judging panel. All solutions are shared within a public forum, with the results of the mission celebrated. Student-led parent–teacher conferences take place at the end of a mission, allowing students to reflect on their work and share their process with their parents.

At the end of semester's Missions and their culminating Boss Levels, a seminar is held with teachers and the advisory board to look at outcomes for the semester. This seminar is moderated by the Institute of Play and serves as a tool for professional development and as a way to maintain the school's vision across a range of stakeholders.

Key Values
- The lack of something becomes a key to solving the Mission: Quests may be designed so that at the beginning students lack needed resources or skills and must acquire them to gain expertise in order to proceed. For example, students may initially lack the ability to convert fractions into decimals, a skill required by a Mission. This lack will encourage students to discover this skill as something they need to learn how to do and will help motivate them to acquire this particular way of knowing.
- Students learn to do something as a *means* to solve a Quest (i.e., "I am learning fractions because I need to know how to work with them in order to address an aspect of the Quest I am working on.")
- If students have difficulty with a Quest, there will be an opportunity for a teacher to redesign the Quest with the students and have them replay it.

Archiving and Documentation of Quests

Discovery Missions, Quests, and Boss Levels provide a curricular infrastructure for building partnerships with external organizations. For example, we might work with the Natural History Museum to build a series of Quests that engage their collections. These Quests will be documented and archived so that teachers can access, share, and use them in different ways each year.

Technology Integration

Q2L's technology integration considers purpose and pedagogy in developing appropriate and affordable technology solutions. The primary educational goal is to integrate technology effectively into the classroom with the purpose of adding breadth and depth to all students' educational experiences. The nature of our academic technology integration is linked directly to Q2L's curriculum and learning objectives. Learning environments that successfully integrate technology afford their students greater opportunities to create and construct knowledge; they also provide teachers with multifaceted resources to aid in the differentiation of curricula. Educational technologies allow students new means of demonstrating their understanding. Students can express themselves as researchers, designers, filmmakers, photographers, songwriters, and engineers. These new means are compelling and assist in the development of skill sets necessary in contemporary professions. Modeling best practices, technology personnel support the classroom teachers' efforts, enabling the teachers to become self-sufficient technology integrators.

What is technology integration, though? Like screwdrivers or space shuttles, high-tech hardware and software are most useful when used for clearly defined purposes. Their power can be unleashed only if we also pay sustained attention to curriculum, school organization, educational philosophies, instructional practices, family and community involvement, and the other components of successful schools.

Educational technology is used as a tool to deepen a student's understanding of a particular subject, concept, or skill and to foster communication within the school and beyond. Applications are chosen based on their ability to model or extend the thinking or problem solving that is central to the classroom. At times, technology is used to imitate what is being done in the classroom, thus reinforcing learning and oftentimes allowing students to move further forward to enhance learning.

Technology integration takes shape in the Q2L classroom in various ways. We provide tools that allow classrooms to collaborate effectively and to produce compelling lessons. Our model designates the classroom teacher as the party responsible for ensuring that the use of technology is compelling and in context. Teachers also act as a front line of support for the technology present in their classroom. The role of the technology group will be to support this approach, scaffolding teachers and thus allowing them to integrate technology ubiquitously and intimately into their work with students.

Q2L technology integrators serve as mentors in both technology and teaching. They support teachers individually and model best practices with technology in the classroom. The support of technology integrators affords teachers successful experiences with technology, which often means that the integrators are in the classroom (virtually or physically) for the duration of Missions and Quests they have helped to plan. Any work they do with teachers is borne of the teachers' own content and style, which allows the teachers a deep connection to and ownership of the project. Individualizing this approach to technology is a key facet to its success with teachers.

Discovery Mission and Quest Design

Discovery Mission and Quest design entails collaboration between teachers, on the one hand, and game design and learning experts in residence at the Institute of Play, on the other. Teachers, working in teams, establish a set of standards, core content, and assessment methods for each unit. Designers from the Institute of Play then work with the teachers to translate this material into Mission and Quest form. Three planning sessions per week are dedicated to this work, and semiannual retreats allow for planning and development.

Discovery Mission Curriculum Template

Box 1

Mission Blurb
Write a short paragraph that describes in simple terms the main problem space students are being dropped into: What is the primary dilemma or problem? What identities or roles will they take on? What does this Mission challenge the students to do, learn, and explore?

Mission Narrative
Write a short paragraph that describes the narrative framing the Mission. The narrative should focus on the "need to know" (i.e., what students need to know) and should provide a clear description of where the students fit into the narrative. This description can be accompanied by a bulleted list of the narrative's core elements.

Box 1

(continued)

Deliverables
Include a bulleted list of possible deliverables that can be developed as part of the Mission.

Assessment
List the types of evidence and tools to be used to maximize documentation of student progress and understandings at formative and summative stages of this Mission (for example: "The following competencies will be evaluated in this Mission: . . .").

Mission Structure
What structure do you think the Mission will take? Will it contain certain stages, phases, or chapters? Does it have a part 1 and a part 2, with a culminating Quest? Is it made up of a series of Quests of similar length? This description will be speculative at first because the details will likely change, but do your best to offer a sense of how the Mission might be structured as a learning sequence.

Overview of Quests: Quick Sketches of Ideas
Create a one-sentence blurb for a series of Quests that you think might make up the Mission. Each quest should have a working title and give a snapshot of the Quest's goal: What are students going to do, and why?

Quest 1: [Title]

Quest Description:

Quest is complete when:

Length:

Essential Question:

Big Idea:

Core Competencies Covered:

Content Covered:

Knowledge:

Skills:

Possible Learning Activities:

Learning Strategies   How are the following to be created for the student?

Need to Know   What "need to know" does the Quest create?

Collaboration   What need does the Quest create in students that requires the sharing of concepts/practices?

Box 1

(continued)

Opportunities for Sharing   What occasions are presented for sharing and reflection during the Quest?

Reflection   What contexts does the Quest create to enable sharing and reflection?

Feedback and Validation   How do students receive feedback and validation on their progress in a Quest?

Dissemination   What channels are activated for dissemination of Quest solutions?

Continuum of Quest Knowledge Assessment
What assessment evidence and tools are needed to support a formative-summative learning cycle?

1. Planning the Quest
What student prior knowledge and experiences—here or elsewhere—can be used to plan the Quest? To kick off the Quest?

2. Doing the Quest
What criteria and tools are particularly apt to capture in situ learning? What criteria will be used to judge the validity and effectiveness of Quest solutions (e.g., speed of solution, creativity or innovation, effectiveness of resource, etc.)?

3. Culminating the Quest
What summative criteria, evidence, and parallel experience forms support judgment about the level of student learning and achievement?

4. Culminating Mission Fluency Assessment
What summative evidence demonstrates student learning on a trajectory from novice to expert fluency?

Teacher's Self-Assessment of Mission Results

Cohesion   *Do Quests fit with the Mission's overarching goal? Is the unit sticky?*

Construct   *Does the Mission structure and its Quests enable students to meet the Mission's stated knowledge domain and standards outcomes?*

Scaffolding   *How did I support student learning given time, place-space, resources, pedagogy, levels of learning (novice-to-expert assessment of progress), and evaluation of learning outcomes?*

Revisioning   *What needs further thought and iterative design for next time? Why?*

Curriculum Directors' Planning Template

Box 2

I. Mission Overview

Overview of Mission Design
What is the purpose of the Mission, key moments in the mission, goals for students learning, and preparation for Boss Level requirements?

Core Understandings (Big Ideas)
What are the enduring understandings? They should include content, domain, and game design/system understandings.

II. Mission Accomplished: Preparation for Future Learning
What evidence will be collected to determine whether the core understandings have been developed, the knowledge and skills attained, and the state standards met? (Anchor the work in performance tasks that involve application, supplemented as needed by prompted work, quizzes, observations, and so on.)

Essential Questions Explored in the Mission	Knowledge and Skills
What arguable, recurring, and thought-provoking questions will guide the inquiry and point toward the Mission's big ideas?	What are the key knowledge and skills needed to develop the desired understandings? What New York State standards are addressed in the mission? What knowledge and skills relate to the content standards on which the Mission is focused?
Assessment Strategies and Culminating Assessment	**Pedagogy: Learning to Be**
What types of evidence and tools will be used to maximize documentation of student progress and understandings at the Mission's formative and summative stages?	What identity and behaviors are students stepping into? How does the mission create: 1. A need to know for students? 2. A need to share between students? 3. Opportunities for feedback and reflection?

Box 2
(continued)

III. Mission Quests: Learning and Assessment Plan
What is the assessment and learning plan for each Quest?

Quest Overview
What is the Quest's goal, and how does this Quest enable students to complete ongoing and cumulative assessment successfully?

Focusing Question
What is the primary question guiding the Quest? How does this question create a space of inquiry for students?

Assessment and Feedback
What are the assessment and feedback tools for the Quest?

Challenge Posed
What is the key challenge students will be asked to solve?

Learning Plan
What sequence of learning experiences will enable students to engage with the core understandings successfully?

Data Set Created, Collected, or Used
What type of data set(s) is at the core of the Quest? How will students use these date to meet the Quest's goals successfully?

Resources
What smart tools will students use to complete the quest?

Scenarios for Potential Uses of Gaming

Students at Q2L play and design games. While they are gaming, they pay explicit attention to the status of games as dynamic learning systems, as rule-based models supporting specific ways of knowing and doing. Beginning in the sixth grade and continuing through the twelfth grade, students gain practice each day in reflecting on the process and practices of learning. Games and the playing of them serve as their primary resources.

Rather than thinking about games and their play generally, however, both students and teachers at Q2L use games in many different ways to support different intentions and purposes.

Games as "Engines" or Authoring Platforms: Authoring Systems
In this scenario, students use games to produce an artifact, be it
a game (*Gamestar Mechanic*), a mod (*Starcraft*), a video (machinima in *WOW*, *SimCity*, *Second Life*, etc.), a visual text (*Sims
Family Album*), an avatar (*Miis*), a written text (*7Scenes*), or a
body of code (*Alice*, *Scratch*). Rubrics for evaluation of these artifacts come not from the game, but from the design domain to
which the artifact is related and from the kinds of understandings the artifact was produced to express. Commercial off-the-
shelf games, Web-based games, and software platforms or
virtual worlds can be used.

Games as Content: Content Systems   In this scenario, commercial off-the-shelf or other games are used to deliver understanding about a particular subject or content area. For example,
students play *SimCity* to learn about urban planning or *Civilization IV* to learn about history. When games are used this way,
students must be provided with opportunities for reflection on
and discussion of the content in spaces external to the game in
order to allow them to see the game as part of a larger body of
knowledge on that subject.

Games as Simulations: Manipulating Systems   In this scenario,
games are valued as dynamic systems with which students can
test theories about how systems work as well as how certain
principles of dynamic systems can be observed and played out.
For example, students may play *Bridge Builder* to learn about
bridges as systems of engineering or use *Soda Play* as a way to
test out physics-based theories. They might play *Animal Cross-*

ing in order to work with elements of a capitalist economy or theater games to reenact situations or scenarios as a way to see how the system can be affected by manipulating certain elements. Simulations often include their own internal assessment measures (data) that can be used to gauge student understanding of both micro and macro elements. Commercial off-the-shelf games, Web-based simulation tools, and downloadable software can be used.

Games as Context: Trigger Systems In this scenario, games are used to create an experiential context for understanding around a topic, issue, or principle that a teacher can build on. For example, a math teacher might have students play *Mafia* as a way to have them experience an ethical dilemma or *Pictionary* as a way to introduce ideas about forms of communication. When games are used this way, students must be provided with opportunities for reflection on and discussion of the content in spaces external to the game in order to allow them to see the game as part of a larger body of knowledge on that subject. Depending on the amount of time available, commercial, casual, and nondigital games can be used. This approach can be paired with the use of games as engines: students can be asked to design a game as a way to become immersed in research around a topic. Later learning experiences can then build on what was learned in order to build a game.

Games as Technology Gateways: Gateway Systems In this scenario, games are used as a way to give students experience with technology, whether it be in learning how to use a particular piece of software or platform (i.e., how to use a personal computer or a browser) or learning how to use a kind of technology (a mobile phone, wireless device). Assessment models are based on a student's effectiveness with and ability to use the system to do what he or she wants it to do.

Games as Illustration: Reflective Systems   In this scenario, games are used as contexts for student reflection. For example, a teacher might ask students to play a game and then discuss the choices they made: why did they choose that avatar skin over another one? Why did they choose to attack that country and not another one? What made them uncomfortable, and what were they surprised at having chosen to do? Commercial off-the-shelf, Web-based downloadable games, and board games can be used.

Games as Exemplars of Point of View: Point-of-View Systems   In this scenario, games allow students to take on certain identities and associated points of view. Students might play a role-playing game where they have to choose to play both a "good" and "bad" character and compare differences in strategy, choice, and values held by those characters. A teacher might ask students to use a theater game to reenact a familiar scenario from several different points of view, with each character's goal being to shift the outcome of the scenario in his or her favor.

Games as Codeworlds: Code Systems   In this scenario, students use writing as the primary mechanic of game play, whether they are playing text adventures or designing or playing text-based mobile games. The emphasis here is in the use of writing as both a mode of action and a mode of expression. Because writing itself is produced as an artifact of the game play, this writing can be assessed to capture student understanding. There is an opportunity to connect this approach to games with the introduction of a programming curriculum that might use authoring platforms, such as *Scratch* or *Alice*, or virtual worlds that support object creation, such as *Second Life*.

Games as Documentary: Documentary Systems   In this scenario, the play of a game is used as documentary evidence of student ideas and understanding. For example, students may be asked to play *SimCity* in such a way as to re-create certain social scenarios that they are interested in. Machinima or storyboarding with screenshots can be used to capture the details of the situation, which then can be used as the basis for additional discussion or reflection. Commercial off-the-shelf and Web-based downloadable games can be used.

Games as Text: Ideological Systems   In this scenario, games are "read" as texts that express certain underlying ideologies, values, beliefs, and so on. In the same way that *Uncle Tom's Cabin* can be read as an expression of the antebellum South, *Animal Crossing* can be played and analyzed as an expression of late-twentieth-century capitalism, *Chess* can be played and analyzed as a game about territorial conflict, and *Diplomacy* can serve as a model of the intricacies of international diplomacy. When games are used this way, students must be provided with opportunities for reflection on and discussion in spaces external to the game and ideally in relation to other media. Commercial off-the-shelf, Web-based downloadable games, board games, and other kinds of nondigital games can be used.

Games as Research: Research Systems   In this scenario, students design games as a research activity that produces material to be used in later learning experiences. Because a designer must be knowledgeable about the system he or she is designing, using game design in this way requires students to think through how their players are learning and what they need to know about the subject of the game. In this way, students not only research material to be used, but also edit this material and are introduced to issues around credibility and point of view. Different kinds of research methods can be introduced as part of the work as well.

Games as Assessment: Assessment Systems   In this scenario, games can be used as environments for assessing student learning of curricular content or state standards. For example, students might play *Quest Atlantis* to show their understanding of certain science concepts, or they might play a *7Scenes* game that centers on answering questions around certain content.

Key Characteristics

School Organization and Structure

Q2L's student population is integrated and diverse. An emphasis in recruiting students is placed on reflecting not only race, but gender, ethnicity, and the attendance area's socioeconomic and academic levels. Attention is also paid to the inclusion of special-education and English-language learners.

Integrated Domains
The Integrated Domains that make up Q2L offer the primary learning contexts for students. Through the structure of Discovery Missions and the culminating Boss Levels, students are provided with rich, integrated contexts in which to practice with a range of ways of knowing, informed by the school's foundation in math and writing as well as state standards. In the sixth grade, each domain class meets a minimum of three times each week.

Choice (XPods)
Q2L teachers are hired in part because they bring a set of passions and interests to bear on the curriculum. Choice courses

are electives created by faculty around topics that support these passions and interests. They allow for smaller class sizes because all teachers in a grade are teaching at the same time. This structure also allows teachers to coteach a larger group of students, to collaborate on a topic, or to do explorations around particular tools or technologies. Choice courses run for six weeks, two Choice sessions per semester. In the sixth grade, Choice classes meet four times each week.

Here are some sample Choice classes:

- Mr. Smiley is a devoted chef and wants to have the students explore cooking. He develops a course where students are challenged to develop menus for the rest of the school based on locally grown food. The students have first to gain an understanding of where the food comes from and make decisions about what can be on the menu at what part of the year. During the last two weeks of the course, students create lunch for the entire school, applying math and science concepts.
- Mrs. Shapiro is a ham radio hobbyist and develops a course to teach students how to run their own ham radio station. She shares students with Miss Torres, who is running a Choice class called "The Wireless Imagination." Students learn how to build pirate radios from found materials, focusing on understanding how electricity and circuits work.
- Mr. Chau is an avid *Dungeons and Dragons* player. He is running a Choice class in *D&D* focusing on methods for calculating probability and the design of narrative scenarios.

Specials
Teachers meet for one hour every day for planning, except for Wednesdays, when they have an additional three hours. During

these periods, students take "Specials": elective classes taught by school partner groups. Specials are opportunities for students to do work in specific areas of curricular interest—Lego Robotics League, Anime Book Club, Civilization League, Spoken Word, and so on— or for one-on-one tutoring of students who may want or need extra help in reading or numeracy. Because we are envisioning the school as a research and demonstration site, Specials play a significant role in creating contexts for research partnerships with universities, corporations, and nonprofits as well as in establishing a context for student internships.

The Mission Annex
Teachers plan and implement a numeracy and literacy-focused enrichment period for students three times each week. The purpose of the Mission Annex is to provide students with a practice and "tinkering" space around key math and ELA concepts related to a domain's Discovery Mission. This period can be used to support students struggling in particular areas of a Mission or to provide extended opportunities for students who are meeting current Mission requirements.

Student Advisory Groups: Home Base
The advisory period—called Home Base—is critical to the development of the culture of success and safety within the school. During this period, held both at the start and at the end of the school day, students have the opportunity to develop a close relationship with a trusted adult who will help create an environment where the student's voice can be heard. The same adult will remain consistently in this position across the seven years of the students' school experience and will know the

student and his or her family well in order to maximize the support provided for student learning and growth. This program is structured around the development of students' academic, personal, and community "voice." Students use Home Base to reflect and plan with their advisers for their continual success.

Professional-development (PD) structures are in place to support teachers in doing advisory, and at the beginning of the year all teachers take part in a workshop focused on student advisories. Goals for the advisory groups include:

- Creating a practice space for community development
- Building deep relationships of trust and mentorship between students and dedicated adults
- Offering a structured time to discuss school issues
- Offering readiness and preparation time: "How ready are we to be good learners?"
- Focusing on disposition development;
- Highlighting and praising student achievements and goals.

Structure of the Day/Week

School begins at 8:00 a.m. and ends for students at 4:10 p.m. on Monday, Tuesday, Thursday, and Friday. On Wednesdays, the day ends for students at 2:00 p.m. to provide PD time for teachers. All students in grades 6 through 12 use the same schedule to enable course acceleration across grade levels. Once the upper school opens, coordination with local colleges and universities will take place to allow students to access college-level courses as part of their class schedules.

The schedule is organized into A, B, and C schedules. Context and Choice classes are will be 80 minutes in length, and Specials are 60 minutes, with 5 minutes allotted for passing between classes.

Schedules A and B: Discovery Missions

Schedules A and B run for 10 weeks each semester. Students follow schedule A on Mondays and Tuesdays and Schedule B on Thursdays and Fridays. Students meet until 2:00 p.m. only on Wednesdays and take elective courses called Choice. During schedules A and B, students are immersed in Discovery Missions delivered within the contexts of the Integrated Domains (The Way Things Work; Sports for the Mind; Being, Space, and Place; Codeworlds; and Wellness.)

Schedule C: Boss Levels

Schedule C runs during the last two weeks of a semester and provides a two-week "intensive" known as a Boss Level, where students and teachers work collaboratively on a capstone project. This project represents a space of defense of skills and competencies acquired during the previous 10 weeks. During a Boss Level, students participate in a rigorous process of research, theory building, hypothesis testing, evaluation, and critique—all followed by a public defense of results. Student-led teacher conferences take place at the end of the capstone project, allowing students, teachers, and parents/caregivers to review student achievement and progress together. Students also work within the Wellness learning context three days a week during schedule C.

During Boss Levels, the Sports for the Mind teacher coordinates teaching and learning efforts. The other teachers take on roles as team leaders for groups of students (approximately

12 students per section). Students are assigned to sections and work with each other in that section to complete the Boss Level challenge. During Boss Levels, students have the opportunity to take on assigned roles—producer, engineer, site planner, ethnographer, writer, and so on, depending on the nature of the challenge. Assigning roles allows students to gain practice with different aspects of working in specialized teams and provides the teacher with clear contexts for assessment.

Sixth-Grade Sample Student Schedules

Schedules A and B (Weeks 1–10 of a Trimester)

Box 3

Time	Monday/ Tuesday	Wednesday	Thursday/Friday
8:00–9:05 a.m.	Morning Lab	Morning Lab	Morning Lab
9:10–9:25 a.m.	Morning meeting	Morning meeting	Morning meeting
9:30–9:45 a.m.	Home Base Advisory	Home Base Advisory	Home Base Advisory
9:50–11:10 a.m.	The Way Things Work (math/ science)	Codeworlds (math/ELA)	Codeworlds (math/ELA)
11:15 a.m.– 12:35 p.m.	Being, Space, and Place (social studies/ ELA)	XPods	Sports for the Mind (game design/digital literacy)
12:40–1:20 p.m.	Lunch	Lunch	Lunch
1:25–2:25 p.m.	SPECIAL	1:25–2:00 p.m. Home Base Advisory	SPECIAL

Box 3

(continued)

Time	Monday/ Tuesday	Wednesday	Thursday/Friday
2:30–3:50 p.m.	Being, Space, and Place (social studies/ ELA)	(early dismissal)	Wellness (health/ physical education)
3:55–4:10 p.m.	Home Base Advisory		Home Base Advisory
4:15–6:00 p.m.	Afternoon Lab (optional + snack)		Afternoon Lab (optional + snack)

Schedule C (Weeks 11–12 of a Trimester)

Box 4

Time	Monday/ Tuesday	Wednesday	Thursday/Friday
8:00–9:05 a.m.	Morning Lab	Morning Lab	Morning Lab
9:10–9:25 a.m.	Morning meeting	Morning meeting	Morning meeting
9:30–9:45 a.m.	Home Base Advisory	Home Base Advisory	Home Base Advisory
9:50–11:10 a.m.	Boss Challenge	Boss Challenge	Boss Challenge
11:15 a.m.– 12:35 p.m.	Boss Challenge	Boss Challenge	Boss Challenge
12:40–1:20 p.m.	Lunch	Lunch	Lunch
1:25–2:25 p.m.	SPECIAL	1:25–2:00 p.m. Home Base Advisory	SPECIAL
2:30–3:50 p.m.	Wellness (Mon.)/Boss Challenge (Tues.)	(early dismissal)	Wellness (Thur.)/ Boss Challenge (Fri.)

Box 4
(continued)

Time	Monday/Tuesday	Wednesday	Thursday/Friday
3:55pm–4:10	Home Base Advisory		Home Base Advisory
4:15–6:00 p.m.	Afternoon Lab (optional + snack)		Afternoon Lab (optional + snack)

The Boss Challenge component of our curriculum operates as a primary space in which students earn qualification badges as they participate in a rigorous process of research, theory building, hypothesis testing, evaluation, and critique—all followed by a public defense of results.

Eighth-Grade Sample Student Schedule

Schedules A and B (Weeks 1–10 of a Trimester)

Box 5

Time	Monday/Tuesday	Wednesday	Thursday/Friday
8:00–9:05 a.m.	Morning Lab	Morning Lab	Morning Lab
9:10–9:25 a.m.	Morning meeting	Morning meeting	Morning meeting
9:30–9:45 a.m.	Home Base Advisory	Home Base Advisory	Home Base Advisory
9:50–11:10 a.m.	The Way Things Work (Earth science)	XPods/Internship	Codeworlds (Integrated Algebra I)

Box 5
(continued)

Time	Monday/ Tuesday	Wednesday	Thursday/Friday
11:15 a.m.– 12:35 p.m.	Sports for the Mind (Building in Virtual Worlds)	XPods/intern- ship	Being, Space, and Place (social stud- ies/ELA)
12:40–1:20 p.m.	Lunch	Lunch	Lunch
1:25–2:25 p.m.	Foreign-Lan- guage Lab	1:25–2:00 p.m. internship	Foreign-Language Lab
2:30–3:50 p.m.	Being, Space, and Place (social studies/ ELA)	(early dismissal)	Wellness (health and physical education)
3:55pm–4:10	Home Base Advisory		Home Base Advisory
4:15–6:00 p.m.	Afternoon Lab (optional + snack)		Afternoon Lab (optional + snack)

Schedule C (Weeks 11–12 of a Trimester)

Box 6

Time	Monday/ Tuesday	Wednesday	Thursday/Friday
8:00–9:05 a.m.	Morning Lab	Morning Lab	Morning Lab
9:10–9:25 a.m.	Morning meet- ing	Morning meet- ing	Morning meeting
9:30–9:45 a.m.	Home Base Advisory	Home Base Advisory	Home Base Advisory
9:50–11:10 a.m.	Boss Challenge	Boss Challenge/ Internship	Boss Challenge

Box 6
(continued)

Time	Monday/ Tuesday	Wednesday	Thursday/Friday
11:15 a.m.– 12:35 p.m.	Boss Challenge	Boss Challenge /Internship	Boss Challenge
12:40–1:20 p.m.	Lunch	Lunch	Lunch
1:25–2:25 p.m.	SPECIAL	1:25–2:00 p.m. Home Base Advisory/In-ternship	SPECIAL
2:30–3:50 p.m.	Wellness (Mon.)/Boss Challenge (Tues.)	(early dismissal)	Wellness (Thur.)/ Boss Challenge (Fri.)
3:55–4:10 p.m.	Home Base Advisory		Home Base Advisory
4:15–6:00 p.m.	Afternoon Lab (optional + snack)		Afternoon Lab (optional + snack)

Professional Development

Teachers report to school at 8:00 a.m. each day and complete their contractual day at 4:10 p.m. to allow time for preparation and before/after-school tutoring. This extended time gives students greater access to teachers so that they can receive needed individual attention. Teachers have either a professional planning period each day or a team meeting period with their grade-level team or the Institute of Play for common planning time. Teachers have 80 minutes a day on four days a week (Monday, Tuesday, Thursday, and Friday) dedicated to PD; on Wednesdays, teachers meet together for 120 minutes. Finally, each teacher is expected to dedicate one Saturday morning per month (three hours) to academic support and tutoring of students.

An integrated and well-supported PD plan is a key component of Q2L. Our PD philosophy is based on the school's core values and practices: teachers engage in prototyping and iteration of their teaching methods and curriculum through the following structures:

• *Lesson Study* This collaborative form of PD is based on a convergence of student needs, teacher needs, school needs, and district needs. Largely teacher driven and teacher run, lesson study consists of the study or examination of teaching practice. Through lesson study, teachers engage in a well-defined process that involves discussing lessons that they have first planned and observed together. This process involves hours of discussion, observation, and planning, and it uses video documentation and analysis as a primary tool set.

• *Mission Lab* This site within the school focuses on collaborative curricular work between teachers and game design experts. The Institute of Play, as a formal partner in the school, hosts sessions in game design, systems thinking, and mission planning.

• *Induction Sessions* Teachers entering the school for its opening in fall 2009 attended a series of "induction" sessions prior to the opening of the school, held in late spring and summer. These sessions continued throughout the year as described earlier and will serve as an ongoing induction space for new teachers coming into the school.

• *Outcome Seminar* At the end of each series of Missions and culminating Boss Levels, a seminar is held with teachers and the advisory board to look at the semester's outcomes. This seminar is moderated by the Institute of Play and serves as a tool for PD as well as a way to maintain the school's vision across a range of stakeholders.

• *Public Sharing* Teachers are encouraged to give papers at conferences and to share their work with other professionals in the field as a way to build, grow, revise, stabilize, expand, and share their approach and methods.

• *Specials Short Course* Instructors for Specials are required to take part in a one-hour short course focusing on the school's values and teaching protocols in order to create consistency for the students across all courses.

Studio Q

Studio Q is integrated and well-supported PD plan and a key component of Q2L. Our PD philosophy is based on the school's core design-based values and practices—teachers will engage in prototyping and iteration of their teaching methods and curriculum on an ongoing basis.

At Q2L, we believe that all teachers, students, parents, and staff members are part of a learning community. Thus, we approach PD from the standpoint that each teacher brings knowledge and experiences that are valuable to the learning community, and we recognize that teachers need to be supported in their growth as teachers and learners.

The term *professional development* is used widely in the education community to refer to any type of activity that is designed to improve teachers' knowledge or skills. In fact, however, it can refer to a vast range of activities from "highly targeted work with teachers around specific curricula and teaching practices to short, 'hit-and-run' workshops" (Elmore 2004, 94–95). At Q2L, we seek to support our teachers in pedagogical growth, but we take a very specific approach to this process. For this reason, we have chosen to call our PD model "Studio Q."

The foundation of Studio Q rests on a philosophy of how members of a school community can best support its teachers' effectiveness and sense of satisfaction. Our philosophy is undergirded by current academic literature and research, which has indicated that PD that is *collaborative, school based, focused on student learning, continuous,* and *embedded in teachers' daily work* is the most successful in changing teacher practice (Elmore 2004; Sagor 2000) as well as in increasing teacher retention and satisfaction (Berg, Donaldson, and Johnson 2005; Fulton, Yoon, and Lee 2005). In addition, our design takes into account the characteristics that the National Staff Development Council has identified as key components of quality PD:

- Organizes adults into learning communities whose goals are aligned with those of the school (teams)
- Requires skillful school leaders who guide continuous instructional improvement
- Requires resources to support adult learning and collaboration
- Uses disaggregated student data to determine adult learning priorities, monitor progress, and help sustain continuous improvement
- Uses multiple sources of information to guide improvement and demonstrate its impact
- Prepares educators to apply research to decision making
- Uses learning strategies appropriate to the intended goal
- Applies knowledge about human learning and change

- Provides educators with the knowledge and skills to collaborate
- Prepares educators to understand and appreciate all students, to create safe, orderly, and supportive learning environments, and to hold high expectations for students' academic achievement
- Deepens educators' content knowledge, provides them with research-based instructional strategies to assist students in meeting rigorous academic standards, and prepares them to use various types of classroom assessments appropriately
- Provides educators with knowledge and skills to involve families and other stakeholders appropriately (from the council's Web site at www.nsdc.org/standards/index.cfm)

Guiding Principles of Studio Q

The Studio Q design team has established a set of principles and questions to guide the planning and implementation of Studio Q at Q2L.

1. Teachers and students should engage in a parallel learning process. Adult functioning must model ideal student functioning.
2. Learning experiences should be
    - immersive;
    - inquiry driven and case based;
    - connected to teachers' daily practice;
    - ongoing, continuous, and purposeful;
    - systems driven;
    - design oriented;
    - engaging and motivating;
    - collaborative to construct communal knowledge;
    - able to capitalize on available digital technologies; and accompanied by constant reflection.

3. There needs to be a careful balance between depth and breadth in terms of the skills, content, and understandings that teachers are expected to learn and enact.

4. The curriculum for teachers should be based on adult learning principles.

5. Teachers need time and space to engage in reflection, dialog, and collaboration. Time must be built into the school schedule for this kind of work.

6. Supervision should be multifaceted and related to Studio Q and should include peer review.

Guiding Questions

1. What does it mean to be a teacher at Q2L?

How do we know what to teach? How do we set clear goals? How do we plan? How do we teach? How do we assess?

2. What does it mean to be a learner at Q2L?

How do we learn about ourselves? How do we learn about our students? How do we act on what we learn? How do we learn how to be more effective learners?

3. What does it mean to be a designer at Q2L?

What does it mean to "design"? What roles do collaboration, reflection, and iteration play in the design process? What does it mean to design gamelike learning experiences?

Six Dimensions of Teacher Development

All of the work in Studio Q is geared toward helping teachers develop the knowledge, skills, and understandings needed to be effective teachers in the Q2L model. We have established six dimensions of teaching and learning that guide the work of Studio Q and the evaluation of our teachers.

1. *Designer* Teachers codesign, implement, and revise gamelike curriculum with game designers and curriculum directors.

2. *Assessor* Teachers design and implement embedded assessment, use data from assessments to evaluate student learning, make adjustments to curriculum based on assessments, and help students set learning goals.

3. *Systems Thinker* Teachers understand the architecture of dynamic systems and are able to think systemically.

4. *Wellness Integrator* Teachers understand the dynamics among their students and between students and other members of the school community. They are able to act on understandings of interpersonal and group dynamics to address students' emotional, academic, physical and nutritional needs.

5. *Technology Integrator* Teachers are able to seek out, identify, and use technology to enhance student learning.

6. *Practitioner* Teachers exhibit exemplary pedagogical practices in areas such as differentiating instruction, integration of content expertise, classroom management, communication with parents, lesson planning, students' engagement in learning, and maintenance of an effective learning environment.

Yearly Goals

At the start of each year, Q2L's directors of curriculum and instruction and executive directors will meet with teachers to go over Studio Q goals. Teachers will then participate in individual meetings where they will determine which goals they would like extra support with for the year. If teachers do not meet their yearly goals, the directors of curriculum and instruction will make a PD plan with teachers for the following year to help them meet their goals.

The following structures will be used to support teachers in meeting their goals:

1. *Weekly Studio Q Sessions*   As teachers move through Studio Q each week, they will be working on developing *artifacts* that show evidence of their movement toward their goals. All of these artifacts are meaningful, relevant, and part of teachers' regular work in Studio Q.

2. *Coaching and Feedback*   The directors of curriculum and instruction, the executive directors, coaches/content experts, other teachers, and the Wellness coordinator may visit teachers' classrooms to give feedback regarding their teaching. This feedback is designed to help teachers in meeting the year's Studio Q goals and is not meant to be evaluative. Whenever feedback is given, the "observer" will write up a feedback report. In addition, the directors of curriculum and instruction will serve as mentors for new teachers at Q2L.

3. *Peer Review*   Teachers will engage in a peer-review process. This process will provide new teachers at Q2L with peer-level support and will be used to identify teachers' areas of strength and areas that need extra support. After the first initial review, teachers will be reviewed every three years. Teachers who have been reviewed will participate as committee members the following year.

4. *Informal Observations*   Administrators may arrange to visit teachers' rooms and observe them teach for short periods of time. The purpose of these informal observations is to give feed-

back to teachers on curriculum and teaching practices in an informal manner. Teachers may request informal observations for feedback in particular areas at any point during the school year. These observations do not go into the teacher's file.

Professional-Development Cycle
- *May 2009*   Begin biweekly induction sessions with new Q2L teachers, run by the Institute of Play.
- *August 2009*   Three-week Teacher's Institute, to overlap with a two-week student bridge program, allowing teachers to devote part days to working with new students in informal contexts.
- *Fall 2009–Spring 2010*   Daily PD sessions and work with Mission Lab.
- *May 2010*   Biweekly induction sessions with new Q2L teachers.

Sample Teacher Schedules

Domain: The Way Things Work (Math/Science) Schedule A (Weeks 1–10 of a Trimester)

Box 7

Time	Monday/ Tuesday	Wednesday	Thursday/Friday
8:00–9:05 a.m.	Morning Lab	Morning Lab	Morning Lab
9:10–9:25 a.m.	Morning meeting	Morning meeting	Morning meeting
9:30–9:45 a.m.	Home Base Advisory	Home Base Advisory	Home Base Advisory
9:50–11:10 a.m.	The Way Things Work (math/ science)	Prep	Prep

Box 7
(continued)

Time	Monday/ Tuesday	Wednesday	Thursday/Friday
11:15 a.m.– 12:35 p.m.	Prep	XPods	The Way Things Work (math/ science)
12:40–1:20 p.m.	Lunch	Lunch	Lunch
1:25–2:25 p.m.	PD/Planning	1:25–2:00 p.m. Home Base Advisory	PD/Planning
2:30–3:50 p.m.	The Way Things Work (math/science)	PD	Wellness (math/ science theme)
3:55–4:10 p.m.	Home Base Advisory	PD	Home Base Advisory

Schedule C (Weeks 11–12 of a Trimester)

Box 8

Time	Monday/ Tuesday	Wednesday	Thursday/Friday
8:00–9:05 a.m.	Morning Lab	Morning Lab	Morning Lab
9:10–9:25 a.m.	Morning meeting	Morning meeting	Morning meeting
9:30–9:45 a.m.	Home Base Advisory	Home Base Advisory	Home Base Advisory
9:50–11:10 a.m.	Boss Challenge (team teaching)	Boss Challenge (team teaching)	Boss Challenge (team teaching)
11:15 a.m.–12:35 p.m.	Boss Challenge (team teaching)	Prep	Boss Challenge (team teaching)
12:40–1:20 p.m.	Lunch	Lunch	Lunch
1:25–2:25 p.m.	PD/Planning	1:25–2:00 p.m. Home Base Advisory	PD/Planning

Box 8
(continued)

Time	Monday/Tuesday	Wednesday	Thursday/Friday
2:30–3:50 p.m.	Wellness (Mon.)/ Boss Challenge (Tues.)	PD	Wellness (Thur.)/ Boss Challenge (Fri.)
3:55–4:10 p.m.	Home Base Advisory	PD	Home Base Advisory

Domain: Being, Space, and Place (Social Studies/ELA) Schedule B (Weeks 1–10 of a Trimester)

Box 9

Time	Monday/Tuesday	Wednesday	Thursday/Friday
9:10–9:25 a.m.	Morning meeting	Morning meeting	Morning meeting
9:30–9:45 a.m.	Home Base Advisory	Home Base Advisory	Home Base Advisory
9:50–11:10 a.m.	Prep	XPods	Prep
11:15–12:35 p.m.	Being, Space, and Place (social studies/ELA)	Prep	Being, Space, and Place (social studies/ELA)
12:40–1:20 p.m.	Lunch	Lunch	Lunch
1:25–2:25 p.m.	PD/Planning	1:25–2:00 p.m. Home Base Advisory	PD/Planning
2:30–3:50 p.m.	Being, Space, and Place (social studies/ELA)	PD	Wellness (social studies/ELA theme)

Box 9

(continued)

Time	Monday/Tuesday	Wednesday	Thursday/Friday
3:55–4:10 p.m.	Home Base Advisory	PD	Home Base Advisory
4:15–6:00 p.m.	Afternoon Lab		Afternoon Lab

Schedule C (Weeks 11–12 of a Trimester)

Box 10

Time	Monday/Tuesday	Wednesday	Thursday/Friday
9:10–9:25 a.m.	Morning meeting	Morning meeting	Morning meeting
9:30–9:45 a.m.	Home Base Advisory	Home Base Advisory	Home Base Advisory
9:50–11:10 a.m.	Boss Challenge (team teaching)	Boss Challenge (team teaching)	Boss Challenge (team teaching)
11:15 a.m.–12:35 p.m.	Boss Challenge (team teaching)	Prep	Boss Challenge (team teaching)
12:40–1:20 p.m.	Lunch	Lunch	Lunch
1:25–2:25 p.m.	PD/Planning	1:25–2:00 p.m. Home Base Advisory	PD/Planning
2:30–3:50 p.m.	Wellness (M)/ Boss Challenge (T)	PD	Wellness (TH)/ Boss Challenge (F)
3:55–4:10 p.m.	Home Base Advisory	PD	Home Base Advisory
4:15–6:00 p.m.	Afternoon LAB		Afternoon LAB

School Calendar and Schedule

The school offers instruction 180 days each year for students. Students coming to the school for the first time participate in a two-week bridge program before they start the school year in order to orient them to the school's thematic and instructional model. The year is organized into three trimesters, each 12 weeks in length.

Class Size and Teacher–Student Loads

Teachers are responsible for knowing well and serving approximately 80 students in the first three years and 100 students thereafter as part of a grade-level team. The decision to start with a smaller student body initially was made to allow for capacity building within this new and highly innovative school model. This team shares these 80–100 students, allowing for consistency of approach, interdisciplinary work, and student accountability for learning across subject areas. The team also targets the needed support services for students and intensive individual and family support for students in need.

In order to maximize the extended learning periods and to offer students deep learning with a great deal of individual attention, average class sizes is targeted at 25 students. Research has shown that this target number allows for the needed differentiation for diversity among students and for the development of a relationship between student and teacher that is central to student success.

Special-education teachers and English-language learner teachers serve as supports for identified students and for all teachers who serve these students' learning needs in both inclusion and pullout settings. These specialized teachers must attend team meetings as needed and meet as a special-needs team to help coordinate intervention strategies for all students. Special-education teachers and English-language learner teachers may at times serve as coteachers within the inclusion classroom settings to provide greater mainstreamed support to students and to model differentiated strategies for mainstreamed classroom teachers.

Teachers also serve as advisers to a smaller group of students (approximately 10 students per group). They are the key advocates for their advisees, supporting them in their educational plans in each year of their attendance at Q2L. Teachers-advisers also serve as the main point of contact for parents or guardians as well as for other teachers who interact with these student and who thus are also providing these students with support and help in problem solving.

Teachers and students are organized into grade-level teams, supporting a culture of collaborative work across disciplines and providing a seamless level of support between students and teachers. Each grade-level team has a grade-level leader who is also a teacher in that grade. In addition, teachers are also members of a knowledge domain cluster guided by one lead teacher. Special-area teachers (e.g., arts, physical education, etc.) also form a specialist cluster led by one teacher. Opportunities exist for cross-team meetings and sharing of ideas as well as cross-grade connections.

Grouping for Instruction

Teachers are grouped in order to maximize the quality of the instructional program while meeting the individual needs of the students both in their classes and in their advisories. Faculty are members of three distinct groups to support their development and the quality of instruction for all students:

Whole Faculty

Because the school is designed as a small school, it is critical that the entire faculty have time to work together to build the culture around the belief system that will help all students reach the outcomes represented in the Student Graduate Profile as outlined in "Quest to Learn Community." Weekly meetings serve to engage the entire faculty as a unit around the important instructional issues that will accelerate all students' success.

Grade-Level Teams

As mentioned previously, each faculty member belongs to a grade-level team that is cross disciplinary and is responsible for approximately 80 students. This team meets at least twice weekly to plan together; design interdisciplinary, game-, and systems-based curriculum opportunities for their students; and devise strategies to meet the needs of all the students for whom the team is responsible. Special-area teachers (arts, technology, and physical education) also form appropriate teams and have the opportunity to participate in grade-level teams when staff meetings regarding specific students or student groups are held. Special-needs teachers (special education, English-language learners) participate in grade-level team meetings on a regular basis.

Learning Context Cluster

Teachers gather at least once a month in discipline-specific groups in order to align curriculum vertically, to align the instruction of context-specific skills and capacities, and to devise strategies to bring game design and systems-based content to their specific context. They also focus on context-based literacy strategies, including identification of domain-based vocabulary and writing structures that will assist all students in successfully accessing each thematic domain. In addition, these groups look at student work, examine teacher assignments, design opportunities for peer visitations, engage in text-based discussions and participate in student shadowing experiences using protocols that can also be used within their classrooms in order to engage students actively around the work.

Student Grouping

Students are grouped to maximize their learning within classrooms. To this end, whenever possible, classrooms are heterogeneous in nature. Within each classroom, students have multiple opportunities to work in cooperative groups that are flexible and designed to support accomplishment of the tasks at hand. When needed, students may be placed in flexible, short-term skills groups within the classroom in order to receive extra attention around a particular area of learning.

The goal is to maximize a student's experiences by making the necessary accommodations that will assist the student in accessing the rigorous, developmentally appropriate content of the classroom. Accommodations may include but are not limited to extra time, personnel that follow students into the classroom, adjusted assignments, extended timelines, technological support services, and so on.

Sample Discovery Mission and Quests

Although a comprehensive curriculum is always a work in progress, this section provides an early sample of two Discovery Missions. Both samples demonstrate the model's potential to support state standards within a gamelike framework.

Box 11

Grade 6	Trimester 2: Making Connections
	Essential Questions
	How do the relationships between elements in a system bring change to that system?
	Quest: Creating Charac- **Domain:** Being, Space, and ter Maps Place (ELA/social studies)
	Length: Three weeks
Quest Overview (written to the student)	In our current Mission about the elements of a story, our storyteller, Calla, has lost her point of view. You discovered this when while reading on of her short stories, "The Lost Ring of Zara." The story began OK, but you noticed by the second chapter that her characters' point of view suddenly disappeared. Without

Box 11
(continued)

<table>
<tr><td>

</td><td>

a point of view, Calla is having trouble inventing her characters and knowing just what they need to do next in the story. The characters are running amok, and she has almost given up! As writers, you've worked hard to understand what a point of view is, how individual points of view are developed, how point of view acts as one component in the system of a story, and why point of view is important. This week you will take another step toward assisting Calla by helping her better understand what part of her story system might be broken.
</td></tr>
<tr><td>

Quest Brief
(written to the student)
Length: One and a half weeks
</td><td>

Continuing to work toward your goal of helping Calla find her point of view, in this Quest you will choose a character from one of the two short stories we have already read, "Baseball in April" by Gary Soto and "The House on Mango Street" by Sandra Cisneros, and create a concept map of one character's point of view. This map will show how point of view is a system whose components work together in a story to help define a character. Remember to include all of the system components that make up a point of view. These components are outlined in the rubric we have been working with and include the voice the character speaks in (first person, second person, or third person), style of speaking (formal or informal, for example), perspective (how they think about the world), character background (events that have shaped their point of view), and consistency (Does the character's point of view create a reliable account of what is going on?). Use your concept-mapping skills to show connections between the different components. Once you have a model for your map, use one of the digital authoring tools we've been working with this year to translate your map into an interactive format to make the system's relationships come alive. Be very deliberate in your choice of technology, phrasing, content, and organization because these maps will be used later to illustrate your evidence of how Calla lost her perspective and where it might be found.
</td></tr>
</table>

Box 11

(continued)

	As you build your theory around Calla's lost point of view and move toward completing this Discovery Mission's final goal, remember that writers have goals for the stories they want to tell. Make sure your map tells the story and that your goal is clear. Use your revising skills to refine your ideas: share your map online with friends, play-test other students' maps, talk to your Digital Youth Network mentors. Collect all of the feedback and use it to iterate your map. We will be sharing the maps at the end of the week on the Digital Youth Network site. Good luck with the Quest!
Performance Assessment Task	Create an interactive concept map of a character's point of view, showing how it works as a system of elements.
Essential Question	How does a change in point of view affect other elements in a story?
Enduring Understandings	A story is dependent on transactions between the narrator, readers, and text—what can be seen, known, felt, and understood. Understanding point of view is a key reading strategy for interpreting text.
Content Knowledge	• Elements of a story: plot, character, setting, description, conflict • Point of view • Short story form
Major Skills	• Reading for understanding • Finding the big idea • Paragraph writing • Identifying themes • Concept mapping • Authoring • Identifying point of view
Differentiation (for use by teacher)	**Individual goals and rewards:** The teacher will develop individual goals with each student for their research. As an incentive, when students achieve the goal, they will get the "reward" of being given a piece of information that students need or give students access to an expert they can pose questions to.

Box 11
(continued)

	Level of readings: The teacher will provide a variety of texts at multiple reading levels so that all students are challenged and supported in their own ways.
	Variation in activities: The unit is filled with activities that enact a variety of learning styles and intelligences. Students will engage in creative, academic, and analytical activities. They will be writing, speaking, and working individually and in groups. The variation in activity allows for all students to experience moments of success and challenge.
Standards (for use by teacher)	**ELA** Standard 1: Students will read, write, listen, and speak for information and understanding. Standard 2: Students will read, write, listen, and speak for literary response and expression. Standard 3: Students will read, write, listen, and speak for critical analysis and evaluation. **Social Studies** Standard 2: Students will use a variety of intellectual skills to demonstrate their understanding of major ideas, eras, themes, developments, and turning points in world history and examine the broad sweep of history from a variety of perspectives. **Applied Learning** A1: Problem solving A2: Communication tools and techniques A3a: Information tools and techniques A3b: Use information technology to assist in gathering, organizing, and presenting information. A4: Learning and self-management tools and techniques
Additional Resources + Digital Tools	Part of becoming an expert Quester means learning to use the resources that are available to you outside this class. Is there an XPod you are taking this week, such as Anime Book Club or Science Explorers, that might help you create your maps? Home Base is another resource you might use. Is there a question you might pose to your mentor or group during your meeting

Box 11
(continued)

that will help you think through a problem you are
struggling with?
Platforms and Tools:
Stella
Omni Graffle
MindMapper
Nova Mind
PhotoShop
Flash
Pages

Box 12

Grade 12	**Trimester 1: Empowering Communities of Change** **Essential Questions** *In what ways does the representation of a dynamic system* *affect our understandings and beliefs about that system?*
	Mission: Decision Making **Domain:** Codeworlds in a Democracy (math/ELA) Length: Six weeks
Quest Overview	The power to elect officials is the power to change the world, but the mathematics of voting extends far beyond the notion of majority rule. As a member of a new grassroots group with a mandate to edu- cate young people about the inner workings of the election process, your mission is to use mathemati- cal models and digital simulations to represent this complex process to others. You must first learn what assumptions they hold about how the election system works: The candidate with the most votes wins an election, for example. It is your job to develop a per- suasive mathematical model to show that the whole story has as much to do with voting methods as with voting numbers. This Math Mission challenges you to grapple with complex questions that are a very real

Box 12

(continued)

	part of our political system, through both mathematical modeling and historical analysis of past elections. (Adapted from the COMAP's Mathematics: Modeling Our World curriculum [Author Date].)
Quest Brief Length: three weeks	The Mathematics of Presidential Elections Number notions underlying the election of the president of the United States can be the source of many "what if" questions. Winning and losing outcomes invariably rest on a straightforward application of the counting process and resulting number comparisons. At first glance, such applications may suggest a simple procedure, but further reflection shows that this simplicity feature fades away. Is it the popular vote that elects the president, or does some other counting scheme apply? What if no candidate receives a majority of the electoral votes cast? Who makes the decision if certain vote totals are in doubt?
Performance Assessment Task	Build a mathematically accurate prediction engine for a hypothetical election.
Essential Question	What is an effective election process?
Enduring Understandings	• Modeling depends on the quality of the measurements collected. • There is value in verifying that mathematical and statistical models make sense both mathematically and contextually. • Systems have dynamics: there are multiple relationships within a system.
Content Knowledge	• Structure of U.S. election process • Advanced algebra • Introduction to mathematical modeling in the context of elections • Feedback loops • Algorithmic modeling
Major Skills	• Mathematical modeling • Analytical reasoning

Box 12
(continued)

	• Number sense and percentages • Understanding of new representations, including preference diagrams and digraphs, and current election-reform topics such as instant runoffs and approval voting; • Ability to use online models and simulations to conduct students' own elections and explore "what if" questions with election data.
Differentiation	**Varied levels:** Students select approach to modeling based on interest, and readings can vary depending on readiness; students offer multiple forms of presentation of final models. **Individual goals and rewards:** The teacher will develop individual goals with each student for his or her research. **Varied outcomes:** Variation in complexity of models that students can produce based on readiness.
Standards	**Mathematics, Science, and Technology** Standard 1: Students will use mathematical analysis, scientific inquiry, and engineering design, as appropriate, to pose questions, seek answers, and develop solutions. Standard 2: Students will access, generate, process, and transfer information using appropriate technologies. Standard 3: Students will understand mathematics and become mathematically confident by communicating and reasoning mathematically, by applying mathematics in real-world settings, and by solving problems through the integrated study of number systems, geometry, algebra, data analysis, probability, and trigonometry. Standard 5: Students will apply technological knowledge and skills to design, construct, use, and evaluate products and systems to satisfy human and environmental needs.

Box 12
(continued)

	Standard 7: Students will apply the knowledge and thinking skills of mathematics, science, and technology to address real-life problems and make informed decisions.
	Social Studies
	Standard 5: Students will apply knowledge in civics, citizenship, and government.
	Applied Learning
	A1a: Design a product, service or system; identify needs that can be met by new products, services, or systems; and create solutions for meeting them.
	A1b: Improve a system; develop an understanding of the way systems of people, machines, and processes work; troubleshoot problems in their operation; and devise strategies for improving their effectiveness.
	A3a: Gather information to assist in completing project work.
	A3b. Use online resources to exchange information for specific purposes.
	A4a. Learn from models.
	A4c. Evaluate one's performance.
Additional Resources + Digital Tools	Multiple resources are available to assist students. The National Election Data Archive and Google's Election Maps Gallery provide sample models.
	COMAP's Election Machine can help students test their models.
	Students can use the open framework library of statistical models they built earlier in the year, which contains modules that will assist them in doing calculations.
	Questions can be posed on the class list-serve.
	Online mentors are available to work with students through Digital Youth Network Mentors.
	A class Web page will contain links to all resources.

Sample Sixth-Grade Mission: The Ways Things Work (Math/Science)

Mission Parameters

Mission Title   Invisible Pathways

Length   10 weeks

Background to Mission   Invisible Pathways follows a 10-week Mission focused on simple machines, which centers on the essential question, "What are the qualities and elements of a system?" and introduces students to science and math-based methods of building simple machines. In this second-trimester Mission, students build on knowledge from the simple-machine unit and apply these understandings to a study of light and matter. The essential question is, "How do the relationships between elements in a system create a dynamic?"

Unit Summary   This Mission casts students in the role of scientists and communication specialists tasked with the job of revealing a message hidden in a beam of light. They will study the interactions of light and matter (refraction, absorption, scattering, and reflection), using digital cameras to document the results. They will use a three-dimensional simulation to model the movement of light through space, applying understandings gained through direct observation in the real world to a virtual representation. They will do data analysis to understand the colors of light and study the eye as an optical device. Throughout the Mission, students will use the scientific method to propose and test theories, observe and gather evidence of outcomes, and apply this understanding to the development of new theories. The Mission will culminate in a scientific challenge requiring students to collaborate in small teams: to construct a pathway for a beam of light to travel to a target, changing direction a minimum of five times. The resulting pathway will require students to apply their understanding of the different ways light interacts with different materials, how it is filtered, strengthened, and changed.

Box 13

STAGE 1: DESIRED RESULTS

Established Goals
New York State Learning Standards for Math, Science, and Technology:
- Students will use mathematical analysis, scientific inquiry, and engineering design, as appropriate, to pose questions, seek answers, and develop solutions.
- Students will access, generate, process, and transfer information using appropriate technologies.
- Students will understand mathematics and become mathematically confident by communicating and reasoning mathematically, by applying mathematics in real-world settings, and by solving problems through the integrated study of number systems, geometry, algebra, data analysis, probability, and trigonometry.
- Students will apply the knowledge and thinking skills of mathematics, science, and technology to address real-life problems and make informed decisions.

Enduring Understandings	**Essential Questions**
Students will understand that	• How does light interact with
• The interaction of elements	matter?
(light and matter) creates a set of	• How do the relationships between
relationships within a system.	elements in a system create a dy-
• The relationships between ele-	namic?
ments in a system can change.	
• Systems are dynamic.	

Science Skills
Students will be able to
- Collect and use data as evidence
- Observe and describe relationships between light and matter
- Mix and separate colors of light

Box 13
(continued)

- Create material models to show how we see an object
- Create concept maps to model relationships in a system
- Make predictions

Mathematics Skills
Students will be able to
- Analyze data
- Calculate supplemental and complementary angles
- Measure angles
- Recognize and identify patterns

Digital Media Skills
Students will be able to
- Use appropriate graphic and electronic tools and techniques to process information.

Knowledge
Students will know
- There are different kinds of interactions between light and matter (refraction, absorption, scattering, reflection).
- The anatomy of the eye.
- How light moves.
- Light from a primary or secondary source must enter the eye in order for the source to be seen. Human eyes can detect only a limited range of light wavelengths.
- Different wavelengths of light are perceived as different colors. Colors of light can be combined or separated to appear as new colors.
- Colored objects selectively reflect, transmit, and absorb different colors of light.
- Shadows are the result of the absence of light.
- Nonvisible light behaves like visible light but cannot be detected by human eyes.
- The difference between supplementary and complementary angles.

STAGE 2: ASSESSMENT EVIDENCE

Performance Task:	Other Evidence:
Digital model (game): During stage 2 of the unit, students will build complex three-dimensional	Online Lab Notebook (Daily) Test Self-assessments

---

Box 13

(continued)

| spaces from simulated light and matter. Culminating assessment (experiment): Students will construct a pathway for a beam of light to travel to a target, changing direction a minimum of five times. | Concept maps
Written reflections |

STAGE 3: LEARNING ACTIVITIES (Quests)

Quest I. The Problem of the Oar (one week total)

Students will develop an inventory of behaviors for "Photon," a beam of light that has lost its way. Using the scientific method, students will produce a series of increasingly complex experiments pairing Photon with a range of materials (water, glass, Plexiglass, mirrors, etc.) to gather data on its behavior. Near the end of this stage, they must decipher an invisible message using only a light. This "secret message" is printed in red and green letters on a black background inside a box. When the message is illuminated with red or green light, only vowels or consonants appear. Only when illuminated with white light will the entire message be visible. Students will document their findings using digital cameras and annotate the resulting images in an online notebook.

Quest II. Enigmo (two weeks total)

Having collected an inventory of behaviors describing Photon's interaction with different forms of matter, students are challenged to apply this knowledge within a three-dimensional simulation tool called "Enigmo 2." This tool allows students to build complex three-dimensional spaces from simulated light and matter. The digital models built by students will be made available for play by other students at Q2L on the school's online network.

Quest III. Can You Believe What You See? (three weeks total)

Students work with a digital model of the eye. Using "light-boxes," they establish the conditions for sight: a light source, an object, an eye, and a straight unblocked path. They are challenged to create material models to show how we see an object. As a result, the students generate questions they would like to answer about light and sort them into four categories: How does light allow me to see? How does light interact

Box 13
(continued)

with matter? How can light have different colors? Is there light that I cannot see? These questions lead the students to understand that light needs to "bounce" from an object to their eyes in order to be seen. But how does light bounce? Does it always bounce? Are there other things it can do?

Quest IV. Invisible Pathways (four weeks total)
The Mission culminates in a Quest requiring students to collaborate in small teams. The challenge: construct a pathway for a beam of light to travel to a target, but changing direction a minimum of five times on its way. The resulting pathway will require students to apply their understanding of the different ways light interacts with different materials—how it is filtered, strengthened, and changed by these materials.

Quest: Light Traveler
Background to Lesson 1   This lesson occurs over two class periods (one hour each) during stage I of the Invisible Pathways Mission. Students develop theories about the ways light can travel as they experiment with different materials to create a light pathway for "Photon," a beam of light who has lost his way. This lesson prepares students for the lesson at the end of Quest I, where they must create a pathway of white light to display a secret message. It also scaffolds their learning so they are prepared for the Mission's final challenge, where they must construct a pathway for a beam of light to travel to a target through a series of complex obstacles.

Box 14

Essential Questions	How does light travel?
	How does light respond to different materials?

Box 14

(continued)

Learning Goals	• Students will identify a technological design dilemma associated with testing how light travels by brainstorming possible ways to observe light using mirrors, prisms, and both clear and clouded materials. • Students will determine procedural sequence, success criteria, and design options to "construct" a light pathway with a single obstacle to investigate how light energy is affected. • Students will begin to develop an understanding of reflection, refraction, absorption, and transmission.
Lesson Objective	**Science/Math Skills** Students will be able to • Identify the ways that light can travel because it is a form of energy. • Design ways to demonstrate the ways that light can travel. • Explain how the ways that light can travel. • Display and analyze data from investigation. • Communicate the findings to explain how light travels. • Generate possible alternative designs for testing light again. • Understand the relationship between complementary and supplementary angles. • Given a vector, calculate the vector's complement.
Digital Platform	Being Me (Q2L online social network), Internet, digital cameras
Learning Sequence and Assessments	1. *Mini-Lesson*: Teacher explains to students that today they will develop an understanding of how light moves so they can get different colors of light to move in the right directions to decipher a secret message. Teacher demonstrates how to investigate properties of light by modeling with a penlight pointer and materials such as mirrors, prisms, and so on. Teacher introduces students to the terms reflection, refraction, absorption, and transmission.

Box 14
(continued)

2. *Investigation*: A small group of students practices with different materials to see how light is affected. For example, they use prisms and see how the prisms refract regular (white) light (from a focused flashlight or another light source) into a rainbow of colors; test mirrors for their capabilities to reflect light; experiment with various materials such as colored filters, waxed paper, clear glass, and translucent (clouded) glass to see how they allow light to travel through. The teacher encourages multiple combinations of materials. Students record their observations in their lab notebooks.

3. *Developing a hypothesis*: Teacher instructs students to examine their data and construct a theory around the behavior of light.

4. *Hypothesis testing*: Students design a light pathway so that light (from a penlight pointer) can travel to a single point through one obstacle. Students sketch out the projected light pathway and predict what will happen at the obstacle. They test their ideas with a penlight pointer to adjust location of their obstacle, through which their final pathway must follow. Adjustments to design are allowed.

5. *Presentation*: Students must display their final light pathway and determine the success of the design based on the class-determined criteria. (Students are required to generate one or more proposals for how to improve their prototype. They may suggest adjustments to the "success" criteria for additional testing.)

6. *Debrief*: Teacher asks students to propose their generalizations about how energy travels, based on what they have learned about light. (Do other forms of energy—heat, sound, electrical and mechanical energy—travel in the same ways as light?). Teacher asks students to revisit the terms introduced at the start of class (reflection, refraction, absorption, and transmission) and asks students to give examples of each term from their experiments. Students record their answers in a graphic organizer.

Box 14

(continued)

Differentia- tion	Each step of the lesson allows for differentiation of instruction. *Step 1*: Teacher modeling. *Step 2*: Guided practice—teacher circulates and works with groups and individuals one on one. *Step 3*: Students work in groups of mixed ability levels to develop hypothesis. *Step 4*: Multiple learning styles are engaged as students test hypothesis. Students are allowed choice in which materials they wish to work with. *Step 5*: Students choose their own job responsibilities for the presentation of their work—some students may be speakers, others demonstrators, others recorders, and so on. *Step 6*: Graphic organizer helps students organize examples of each term.

Box 15

Assessment Culminating Performance Task	**Invisible Pathways:** Construct a pathway for a beam of light to travel to a target, but changing direction a minimum of five times. Experiment: Demonstration—a beam of light changes direction five times, each helping it to reach its target. You have the opportunity to take four trial runs, brainstorming alternative designs to make your light path hit five targets. **Visual map:** Graphical representation (diagram, concept map) of the structure, flow, and spatial relationships of pathways of light and matter in your experiment. This is your vision: be creative about how you conceive of it and what digital tools you use. **"My Inquiry" essay:** A narrative synthesizing your scientific reasoning, procedure, and reflection on being a team member. Include data and examples from your online lab notebook and team experience. Place your drafts and final essay in your "Being Me" networking site for feedback and comments. (Essay: five to seven pages)

School Design Team

The bulk of the work for Q2L to date has been completed by members of the core team, with ongoing work to be supported in an increased capacity by our cadre of core advisers.

Q2L is an ambitious undertaking that has required (and will continue to require) a development process drawing on the experience and expertise of many different individuals. This process has been highly collaborative, reflective, and research driven, and it is currently led by a small core team, which is responsible for the material presented in this proposal. In addition to the core team is a larger group of advisers who serve as sounding boards and who will play an increasingly critical role as we move forward. In future phases of the development process, we anticipate bringing on more expert teachers to guide curriculum development, a number of parents representing community and parenting concerns, and students drawn from populations of the school programs we have been working with to pilot platforms and pedagogy.

Core Design Team

Katie Salen, Institute of Play and Parsons the New School for Design Katie Salen is the executive director of the Institute of Play and Professor, Design and Technology, at Parsons the New School for Design. Coauthor of *Rules of Play: Game Design Fundamentals* (2003), a textbook on game design, as well as *The Game Design Reader* (2005), she is currently working as lead designer on a digital game developed to teach game design to middle school and high school youth. She recently served as editor for the volume *The Ecology of Games* (2007) for the MacArthur Foundation series Digital Media and Learning and is coeditor of the *International Journal of Learning and Media*. She writes extensively on game design, design education, and game culture, including authoring some of the first dispatches from the previously hidden world of machinima.

Robert Torres, Design by Design Robert Torres has worked as a teacher, school principal, and education consultant since 1988. His work has focused mostly on school design, and he currently runs a not-for-profit business that designs small progressive high schools across New York City. Robert wrote and produced a documentary film on the impact of poverty on his Puerto Rican family in New York. The film, *Nuyorican Dream*, premiered at the Sundance 2000 Film Festival, was acquired by and aired on HBO, and has won numerous awards in the United States and abroad. The documentary offers observations about the legacy of colonialism, the inadequate American inner-city educational system, and discrimination. Robert has a master's degree in policy and school administration from Bank Street College of Education and was a Stanford University research fellow. He is currently pursuing a doctorate at New York University focused on games and learning.

Rebecca Rufo-Tepper, East Side Middle School Rebecca Rufo-Tepper has been working in the New York City public-school system for eight years. She is currently a literacy coach at East Side Middle School, a public school in Manhattan, where she previously taught eighth-grade humanities for five years. Rebecca is a professional development facilitator for the Holocaust Educators Network in New York City and the Folger Shakespeare Library in Washington, D.C. She has published a teaching guide with Simon & Schuster for Nathaniel Hawthorne's *The Scarlet Letter* and has worked with PBS on developing lesson plans for its *In Search of Shakespeare* series. She is also a doctoral student in the Urban Education program at the Graduate Center, the City University of New York, where her research focuses on a professional development model known as "Japanese lesson study."

Arana Shapiro, Flat Toads Arana Shapiro has been working in the field of education for ten years. Her first teaching position was in the Inglewood Public School District (California), where she taught for three years. In Inglewood, she served on the district curriculum review team helping to develop and implement new curriculum in this small district. Upon moving to New York City, Arana began working at Teachers College, Columbia University's Early Childhood Education Program. At Teachers

College, she helped develop the Early Childhood Education Department's new student teacher program by visiting New York City public-school classrooms and finding appropriate placement and mentorship for Teachers College students. It was during her work at Teachers College that she began working with a group of educators to develop curriculum for a new school, The School at Columbia University, and subsequently became a founding faculty member of The School in 2003. Arana's desire to bring new media technologies into the classroom prompted her to migrate from the classroom to the technology team at The School and later to the lead educational technologist position at the Ross Institute, where she integrated technology into K–12 classrooms at both the Ross School in East Hampton and the Ross Global Academy Charter School.

Loretta Wolozin, Parsons the New School for Design   Loretta Wolozin, educator, designer, and hockey mom, teaches and coordinates the research and writing curriculum for the master's in design and technology at Parsons the New School for Design. Long ago, when there were no jobs for teachers, she put her teacher's credential and English literature master's to work as education editor for more than twenty-five years at Houghton Mifflin (Boston). She built the K–12 Teacher Education list, collaborating closely with authors on print and media publications, from acquisitions through production. Her article "Look—Duck Feet: Kinderboard on Kindertable Goes to Classrooms," in *TIES: The Online Magazine of Design and Technology Education* (www.tiesmagazine.org/archives/dec_2002/), describes her experience as design researcher and participant testing a novel, table-top installation prototype in two New Jersey public elementary schools.

Core Advisers

Robert L. Hughes, New Visions for Public Schools Robert L. Hughes was appointed president of New Visions in June 2000. A prominent lawyer, he formerly served as deputy director of the Campaign for Fiscal Equity, a coalition of parent organizations, community school boards, concerned citizens, and advocacy groups that seeks to reform New York State's education finance system to ensure adequate resources and the opportunity for a sound basic education for all students in New York City.

Gloria Rakovic, New Visions for Public Schools Gloria Rakovic joined New Visions in 2002 after having served as a principal in urban and suburban environments, including three public New York City high schools. Dr. Rakovic has an extensive background in high school redesign, alternative education, and group facilitation. She helped found and served as principal of both Park East High School and the High School of Telecommunication Arts and Technology.

James Paul Gee, Arizona State University James Paul Gee, formerly the Tashia Morgridge Professor of Reading at the University of Wisconsin–Madison, is the Mary Lou Fulton Professor of Literacy Studies at Arizona State University. His latest book, *Why Video Games Are Good for Your Soul* (2005), shows how good video games marry pleasure and learning and have the capacity to empower people.

Mizuko Ito, University of Southern California   Mizuko (Mimi) Ito is a cultural anthropologist of technology use, focusing on children and youths' changing relationships to media and communications. Her research group at Keio University studies mobile phone use, and she is working with Peter Lyman, Michael Carter, and Diane Harley on a multiyear project concerning digital kids and informal learning, with support from the MacArthur Foundation.

Nichole Pinkard, University of Chicago, Center for Urban School Improvement   Nichole Pinkard is a senior research associate (assistant professor) at the University of Chicago's Center for Urban School Improvement, where she serves as director of technology for the center and as director of the Information Infrastructure System project. Dr. Pinkard plays a leading role in the Urban School's engagement in the ongoing process of researching problems around the integration of advanced technology systems into urban schools.

References

Anderson, J. R., L. M. Reder, and H. A. Simon. 1996. "Situated Learning and Education." *Educational Researcher* 25, no. 4:5–11.

Assaraf, O. B-Z., and N. Orion. 2005. "Development of System Thinking Skills in the Context of Earth System Education." *Journal of Research in Science Teaching* 42, no. 5:518–560.

Berg, J., M. Donaldson, and S. Johnson. 2005. *Who Stays in Teaching and Why. The Project on the Next Generation of Teachers.* Cambridge, Mass.: Harvard Graduate School of Education.

Bransford, J. D., A. L. Brown, and R. R. Cocking, eds. 2000. *How People Learn: Brain, Mind, Experience, and School.* Washington, D.C.: National Research Council, National Academy of Sciences.

Bridgeland, J. M., J. J. DiIulio, and K. B. Morison. 2006. *The Silent Epidemic: Perspectives of High School Dropouts.* Washington, D.C: Civic Enterprises.

Brown, J. S., A. Collins, and P. Duguid. 1991. "Situated Cognition and the Culture of Learning." In *Artificial Intelligence and Education*, ed. M. Yazdani, 32–42. Norwood, N.J.: Ablex.

Christoph, J. N., and M. Nystrand. 2001. "Taking Risks, Negotiating Relationships: One Teacher's Transition toward a Dialogic Classroom." *Research in the Teaching of English* 36, no. 2:249–286.

Delandshere, G. 2002. "Assessment as Inquiry." *Teachers College Record* 104, no. 7 (October):1461–1484.

Driscoll, M. P. 2005. *Psychology of Learning for Instruction*. 3rd ed. Boston: Pearson Education.

Elmore, R. 2004. *School Reform: From the Inside Out*. Cambridge, Mass.: Harvard Education Press.

Federation of American Scientists. 2006. "Harnessing the Power of Video Games for Learning." Paper presented at the Summit on Educational Games, October 25, 2006, Washington, D.C.

Friedman, T. L. 2006. *The World Is Flat*. New York: Farrar, Straus, Giroux.

Fulton, K., I. Yoon, and C. Lee. 2005. *Induction into Learning Communities*. Report published by NCTAF. Retrieved October 25, 2007, from www.nctaf.org/documents/NCTAF_Induction_Paper_2005.pdf

Gee, J. P. 2007. *Good Video Games + Good Learning*. New York: Peter Lang.

Gee, J. P. 2003. *What Video Games Have to Teach Us about Literacy and Learning*. New York: Palgrave Macmillan.

Greene, J. P. 2002. *High School Graduation Rates in the United States*. New York: Center for Civic Innovation at the Manhattan Institute.

Jenkins, H., K. Clinton, R. Purushotma, A. J. Robinson, and M. Weigel. 2006. *Confronting the Challenges of Participatory Culture: Media Education for the 21st Century*. Chicago: John D. and Catherine T. MacArthur Foundation.

Klopfer, E. 2008. *Augmented Learning*. Cambridge, Mass.: MIT Press.

Lave, J. 1990. "The Culture of Acquisition and Practice of Understanding." In *Situated Cognition: Social, Semiotic, and Psychological Perspectives*, ed. D. Kirshner and J. A. Whitson, 17–36. Mahwah, N.J.: Lawrence Erlbaum.

Lave, J., and E. Wenger. 1991. *Situated Learning: Legitimate Peripheral Participation (Learning in Doing: Social, Cognitive and Computational Perspectives).* Boston: Cambridge University Press.

Lenhardt, A., and M. Madden. 2005. *Teen Content Creators and Consumers.* Washington, D.C.: Pew Internet and American Life Project.

Menn, D. 1993. "Multimedia in Education: Arming Our Kids for the Future." *PC World* 11:52–60.

New London Group. 1996. "A Pedagogy of Multiliteracies: Designing Social Futures." *Harvard Educational Review* 66, no. 1:60–92.

Perkins, D. N. 1986. *Knowledge as Design.* Hillsdale, N.J.: Lawrence Erlbaum.

Policy Studies Associates. 2006. *Evaluation of the New Century High Schools Initiative: Report on the Third Year.* Washington, D.C: Policy Studies Associates.

Roberts, D. F., U. G. Foehr, and V. Rideout. 2005. *Generation M: Media in the Lives of 8–18 Year-Olds.* Washington, D.C.: Henry Kaiser Family Foundation.

Sagor, R. 2000. *Guiding School Improvement with Action Research.* Alexandria, Va.: ASCD.

Salen, K., ed. 2007a. *The Ecology of Games: Connecting Youth, Games, and Learning.* Cambridge, Mass.: MIT Press.

Salen, K. 2007b. "Gaming Literacies: A Game Design Study in Action." *Journal of Educational Multimedia and Hypermedia* 16, no. 3:301–322.

Salvia, J., and J. Ysseldyke. 2007. *Assessment 10/e.* Boston: Houghton Mifflin.

Sawyer, R. K. 2006b. "Introduction: The New Science of Learning." In *The Cambridge Handbook of the Learning Sciences,* ed. R. K. Sawyer, 1–18. Cambridge, UK: Cambridge University Press.

Schön, D. 1987. *Educating the Reflective Practitioner.* San Francisco: Jossey Bass.

Shaffer, D. W. 2006. *How Computer Games Help Children Learn.* New York: Palgrave Macmillan.

Squire, K. 2005. "Changing the Game: What Happens When Video Games Enter the Classroom." Retrieved August 23, 2007, from http://www.innovateonline.info/index.php?view=article&id=82.

Squire, K. 2006. "From Content to Context: Videogames as Designed Experience." *Educational Researcher* 35, no. 8:19–29.

Squire, K. D. 2004. *Replaying History: Learning World History through Playing* Civilization III. Bloomington: Indiana University Press.

Torres, R. 2009. "Learning on a 21st Century Platform: Gamestar Mechanic as a Means to Game Design and System Thinking Skills within a Nodal Ecology." Ph.D. diss., New York University.

Wertsch, J. V. 1998. *Mind as Action.* New York: Oxford University Press.

Printed in the United States
by Baker & Taylor Publisher Services